SENIOR INDIVIDUAL ACCOUNTABILITY IN THE FINANCIAL SERVICES ARENA – A PRACTICAL GUIDE

David Berman

Published in March 2017
by Thomson Reuters. Registered in England & Wales,
Company No 1679046. Registered Office and address
for service: 5 Canada Square, Canary Wharf,
London E14 5AQ

A CIP catalogue record for this book is available from the British Library.

ISBN: 9780414063860

Thomson Reuters and the Thomson Reuters logo are trade marks
of Thomson Reuters. Latham & Watkins and the Latham & Watkins
logo are trade marks of Latham & Watkins.

Crown copyright material is reproduced with the permission of the Controller of
HMSO and the Queen's Printer for Scotland.

CONTENTS

Acknowledgements

I am indebted to my wife, Debbie, and my children, Aaron, Eva and Georgia Grace, for their continued support and encouragement, not to mention patience. This book is dedicated to you.

Disclaimer

While it is hoped that this publication serves as a helpful practical guide for senior officers, it does not constitute legal advice. Every situation faced by a senior officer in practice will be characterised by its own particular set of facts and circumstances. Accordingly, professional advice should be sought in specific cases.

PREFACE

While several years have now passed since the global banking crisis, the media and political clamour for more demonstrable senior individual accountability shows no signs of abating. In the wake of the recent LIBOR and FX scandals, the Regulator remains under sustained pressure to deliver on its public commitment to sanction more senior individuals for perceived misconduct.

Historically, the Regulator has famously struggled to bring numerous prominent senior executives (including some of the alleged architects of the banking crisis) to account. It has proven impossible, evidentially, for the Regulator to establish the requisite personal culpability – with the senior manager(s) concerned often situated many operational levels away from the actual scene of the misconduct or issue – and to successfully argue that they were not responsible.

In response to heavy public criticism, the Regulator can be seen to have modified its approach to individual accountability – most obviously, with its increased usage of attestation requests and a new-found reliance on cultural attribution. From March 2016, the Regulator has had a further string to its bow, in the guise of the Senior Managers Regime (SMR).

This publication takes a purposefully practical approach to the topical subject of individual accountability, and follows on from the author's title *Individual Accountability Under the Senior Managers Regime – A Practical Guide* (Thomson Reuters, 2016). The book aims to ensure that senior-level individuals working within regulated financial institutions are well equipped to understand the nature and extent of their regulatory responsibilities and potential liability, and the ways in which this personal exposure can be managed in practice.

This book is of direct relevance to – and designed as a one-stop practical guide for – senior officers of financial services institutions, including those individuals designated as Senior Managers under the SMR (in both executive and non-executive capacities).

While the technical focus of this publication is the UK Senior Managers Regime, much of the underlying guidance will have broader practical application and utility in the context of the US and other prominent regulatory regimes.

In a widely anticipated development, the Regulator has announced that, as from 2018 (precise date yet to be confirmed), the SMR will be rolled out "proportionately" beyond banks and insurers to all UK-regulated firms.

At the time of publication, we know little more than that *"proportionality will play a key role as we [the Regulator] work to ensure the [SMR] works well across all sectors"*. Unsurprisingly, and however the proportionality principle will be applied in practice, *"the tenets of the regime – clarity, accountability and transparency – will not change. Our [the Regulator's] expectations around conduct, whether the firm is large or small, will remain high".*[1]

Accordingly (and importantly), the substantive guidance contained in this book is likely to hold good – regardless of how the proportionality concept is eventually applied in practice.

David Berman 2017

---

[1]   'Getting Culture and Conduct Right – The Role of the Regulator', speech by Jonathan Davidson, FCA Director of Supervision, July 2016.

GUEST FOREWORD

Individual accountability in the financial services industry is, and will likely remain, an area of sustained regulatory focus – not only in the UK and the EU, but across the Atlantic and beyond. Regulators have been much criticised for their perceived inability to sanction those senior-level individuals who presided over institutions embroiled in recent scandals, such as FX and LIBOR.

In response, the UK Senior Managers & Certification Regime (SM&CR) was introduced in 2016 to facilitate the regulator's pursuit of culpable senior managers of banks and insurers. Fundamentally, the SM&CR was designed to equip the regulator with the necessary tools to overcome the often insurmountable evidential hurdles encountered in the past – in particular, lack of clarity over responsibility and accountability gaps.

The SM&CR is scheduled to be rolled out proportionately across the entire financial services industry as from 2018. This will, arguably, represent the single most significant regulatory development for those running firms. Expectations of directors and senior managers have never been more in focus; and the attendant prospect of personal regulatory exposure is certainly serving to concentrate the minds of those concerned.

This publication benefits from the unique (and decidedly practical) perspective of its author – a senior advisory practitioner with extensive industry and private practice experience. Thought-provoking and insightful, this easy-to-read guide serves as an invaluable reference point for senior managers, and directly addresses key areas of concern and uncertainty.

In the current regulatory environment – with its newly heightened focus on individuals very much a reality – this book might well be regarded as the 'standard issuance' for all Senior Managers.

Chris Cummings

Chief Executive, The Investment Association

1

INTRODUCTION

"The accountability of individuals in positions of responsibility needs to be improved and overall standards of governance raised. [The new Senior Managers Regime] will make it easier for both firms and regulators to hold individuals to account."[2]

Backdrop

Senior-level officers of financial institutions are now (and will likely remain) firmly under the regulatory spotlight, facing an unprecedented threat of adverse scrutiny.

The financial services industry has recently witnessed a marked increase in the number of attestation requests by the Regulator, and the new-found phenomenon of culture-based enforcement (referred to for present purposes as 'cultural attribution') against senior individuals. The Senior Managers Regime (SMR) is intended to further facilitate the Regulator's pursuit of individuals for perceived regulatory failings.

Objectives

This book identifies the most likely sources of personal regulatory exposure for senior officer holders within financial institutions, and considers how these risks can be effectively mitigated in practice. In doing so, the book addresses some of the key questions preoccupying senior officers in today's increasingly challenging regulatory environment, including:

- What does the Regulator expect of me?
- What is the scope of my regulatory responsibility?
- What, if any, responsibility do I have for the firm's culture?

---

[2] FCA Business Plan 2015/16.

- To what extent can I be held accountable for the (in)actions of others?
- In what respects/where am I most exposed, from a regulatory perspective? What are the Regulator's most likely avenues of challenge?
- How do I satisfy my Duty of Responsibility, if need be?
- How can I best protect myself and keep the Regulator at bay?
- How can I reconcile my statutory/fiduciary duties as a director with my regulatory responsibilities?
- What assurances should I receive before signing an attestation?
- How should I approach regulatory interviews?

This book is intended as a practical reference guide for senior-level individuals, and is entity-form neutral. While, technically, the SMR applies differentially to UK-based EEA and non-EEA (third country) branches, the key underlying messages and guidance contained in this publication are nevertheless of universal application – irrespective of entity form. Accordingly, this book does not explicitly distinguish between the 'main' and branch variants of the Senior Managers Regime.

Whilst this publication does not expressly account for the nuances of the Senior Insurance Managers Regime, the substantive guidance contained in this edition will likely be of direct relevance to senior individuals operating within that regime.

Similarly, while the technical focus of this book is the UK Senior Managers Regime, much of the underlying practical guidance will have broader application and utility in the context of the US and other prominent regulatory regimes.

Outline

Chapter 2 outlines the key features of the SMR, from the perspective of a Senior Manager. Chapter 3 identifies the various sources of personal regulatory liability for Senior Managers. Chapter 4 addresses how such personal exposure might be managed in practice, with a primary focus on executive role holders. Chapter 5 focuses exclusively on the position of non-executive directors. The topical subjects of culture and attestations, and the associated enforcement risks, are discussed in chapters 6 and 7, respectively. Chapter 8 attempts to reconcile the tension between a director's legal duties and his or her regulatory responsibilities. Chapter 9 suggests a number of practical pointers, followed by some 'real-life' scenarios; and chapter 10 concludes.

Reader notes

Senior Managers holding **non-executive** roles can skip section A of chapter 4 (which is focused on executive role holders).

Senior Managers holding **executive** roles can skip chapter 5 (Non-executive Directors).

For **senior officers of financial institutions regulated in the US and other prominent jurisdictions**, chapters 4, 6 and 9 are likely to be of particular relevance.

Glossary

The term **Regulator**, used throughout this publication, encapsulates both the Financial Conduct Authority (FCA) and the Prudential Regulation Authority (PRA) (as appropriate).

2

THE SENIOR MANAGERS REGIME (SMR)

Introduction

In June 2012, Parliament established the Parliamentary Commission on Banking Standards (PCBS). The purpose of the PCBS was to consider and report on:

- professional standards and culture of the UK banking sector, taking account of regulatory and competition investigations into the LIBOR rate-setting process; and

- lessons to be learned about corporate governance, transparency and conflicts of interest, and their implications for regulations and for government policy.

The PCBS concluded that public trust in banking was at an all-time low, and recommended a series of measures to restore trust and improve culture. Based on these recommendations, the PCBS proposed a new framework for approving individuals and holding them to account, which would include:

- a Senior Persons Regime, to replace the Significant Influence Function (SIF) element of the Approved Persons Regime for deposit-takers and PRA-designated investment firms, with designated Senior Management Functions, covering a narrower range of very senior level individuals;

- a licensing regime (the Certification Regime) operating alongside the Senior Persons Regime and applying to other bank staff whose actions or behaviour could significantly harm the bank, its reputation or its customers; and

- replacing the existing Statements of Principle and Code of Conduct for Approved Persons with a set of enforceable Conduct Rules, which would apply to a wider range of employees than those subject to regulatory approval.

The Financial Services (Banking Reform) Act 2013 (the Act) adopted these central recommendations in the changes it made to the Financial Services and Markets Act 2000 (FSMA). The Act created the legislative framework that underpins the SMR.

Additionally, the Act gave the Regulator enhanced powers when approving, and taking enforcement action against, Senior Managers. These include the ability to impose conditions and time limits on approvals, a new statutory duty for Senior Managers to take reasonable steps to prevent a regulatory contravention from occurring within their area of responsibility (the Duty of Responsibility) and a new criminal offence relating to decisions that cause a financial institution to fail.

A Senior Management Function is defined as:

*"A function that will require a person performing it to be responsible for managing one or more aspects of the relevant firm's affairs, so far as relating to regulated activities, and those aspects involve, or might involve, a risk of **serious consequences** for the authorised person, or for the business or other interests in the UK."*

The SMR contains a number of concepts designed to promote a clear allocation of responsibilities to Senior Managers and, significantly, to **enhance their individual accountability**:

- a requirement for applications for approval as a Senior Manager to contain or be accompanied by a statement setting out the aspects of the firm's affairs that it is intended that the person will be responsible for managing in performing the function (Statement of Responsibilities). A Statement of Responsibilities must be resubmitted whenever there is a 'significant change' in the Senior Manager's responsibilities;

- a requirement for firms to produce and maintain a Responsibilities Map, setting out their overall framework for the allocation of responsibilities to individuals and their governance and management arrangements;

- new statutory powers for the Regulator to impose conditions and time limits on approvals of Senior Managers, both at the initial approval stage and subsequently through a variation of approval;

- new conduct rules applicable to Senior Managers (which closely resemble the former Statements of Principle for Approved Persons);
- if a firm contravenes a relevant requirement, the Senior Manager responsible for the area where the contravention has occurred could be held accountable if the Regulator can prove that they have failed to take 'reasonable steps' to prevent or stop the contravention (Duty of Responsibility; discussed further in chapter 3); and
- potential criminal liability under a new offence relating to a reckless decision causing a financial institution to fail.

The intended combined effect of the Statement of Responsibilities and the Responsibilities Map is to minimise the potential for overlaps and underlaps in accountability, and, in turn, to preclude a relevant Senior Manager from pleading a 'not my responsibility' defence.

Application of the SMR

As widely predicted (and as another by-product of the Bill), the SMR will eventually be rolled out across the entire financial services industry – applying (to (amongst others) investment firms, asset managers, insurance firms,[3] mortgage brokers and consumer credit firms. This will result in the wholesale replacement of the Approved Persons Regime. It is currently envisaged that this broader roll-out will occur during 2018.

According to HM Treasury,[4]

"the key features of the regime [SMR] will be as applied to the banking sector. The principle of proportionality will be particularly important as the [SMR] is extended to a broader range of firms operating in the financial services industry. The regulators will ensure that the extended regime appropriately reflects the diverse business models operating in the UK market and is proportionate to the size and complexity of firms."

---

[3] For insurance firms, *"the introduction of the Senior Insurance Managers Regime will pave the way for the application of the [SMR] to insurers"*. 'Senior Managers and Certification Regime: Extension to all FSMA Authorised Persons', HM Treasury, October 2015.

[4] 'Senior Managers and Certification Regime: Extension to all FSMA Authorised Persons', HM Treasury, October 2015.

While it remains to be seen how the concept of proportionality will actually be reflected in the new rules, it is clear that *"the tenets of the regime – clarity, accountability and transparency – will not change"*.[5] Accordingly (and importantly), the substantive guidance contained in the book is likely to hold good – regardless of how the proportionality concept is eventually applied in practice.

5 'Getting Culture and Conduct Right – The Role of the Regulator', speech by Jonathan Davidson, FCA Director of Supervision, July 2016.

Senior Management Functions (SMFs)

The Regulator has designated the following roles as SMFs:

Function	Reference	FCA/PRA
Chief Executive	SMF1	PRA
Chief Finance	SMF2	PRA
Executive Director	SMF3	FCA
Chief Risk	SMF4	PRA
Head of Internal Audit	SMF5	PRA
Head of key business area	SMF6	PRA
Group Entity Senior Manager	SMF7	PRA
Credit Union SMF (small credit unions only)	SMF8	PRA
Chairman	SMF9	PRA
Chair of Risk Committee	SMF10	PRA
Chair of Audit Committee	SMF11	PRA
Chair of Remuneration Committee	SMF12	PRA
Chair of Nominations Committee	SMF13	FCA
Senior Independent Director	SMF14	PRA
Compliance Oversight	SMF16	FCA
Money laundering reporting	SMF17	FCA
Other overall responsibility	SM18	FCA

Head of key business area (SMF6)

This function is intended to capture those individuals managing a business area or division so large in relative terms to the size of the firm that it could jeopardise its safety and soundness, and so substantial in absolute terms that it warrants an SMF, even though the Senior Manager performing it may report to the Chief Executive or another Senior Manager.[6]

---

[6] An individual will require approval as SMF6 if they manage an area with gross total assets of £10bn or more which accounts for either 20% or more of the firm's or, where the firm is part of a group, 20% of the group's gross revenue.

Multiple approvals

Individuals performing more than one SMF will require separate approvals for each, although these may be combined in a single application.

Shared SMFs

As a general matter, the Regulator expects firms to nominate for each SMF the most senior individual responsible for managing or overseeing that aspect of the firm's affairs. In some cases (only *"where appropriate and justified"[7]*), however, such as a job share, it may be possible for a firm to have more than one individual approved to perform the same SMF. In such a situation, each of the approved individuals will be accountable for *all* the responsibilities conferred by that SMF. Consequently, each may be required to show that they have taken reasonable steps to prevent a breach from occurring or continuing in the management area covered by that SMF.

Senior Managers based in a parent or group entity

Under the Approved Person Regime, an individual who is employed in the parent or other group entity of a relevant firm but who is deemed via an arrangement with the firm to exercise 'significant influence' over its affairs is subject to approval.

This concept will continue under the SMR. Individuals not directly employed by a relevant firm but whose influence over it meets the relevant test must be specifically approved as a Group Entity Senior Manager (SMF7). However, the SMR only applies to a firm's UK-regulated activities. While this inherently limits the extent to which it can apply to individuals in a firm's parent or group entities (particularly those based overseas), the fact that an individual is located outside of the UK does not, in itself, mean that he or she cannot perform an SMF on behalf of the firm.

The Regulator does not require pre-approval of senior individuals located overseas whose responsibilities in relation to the UK are limited to the group's overall strategy. The Regulator's focus is on

---

7   Paragraph 2.10, SS28/15.

those individuals who, irrespective of their location, are directly responsible for implementing the group's strategy in relevant UK firms. Consequently, if an individual based overseas is directly responsible for taking decisions about how a relevant UK firm should conduct its UK-regulated activities and has not delegated this responsibility to a Senior Manager based in the UK, it is likely that he or she will require approval as SMF7.

The Regulator does not aim or expect to approve individuals as SMF7 in every relevant UK firm which is part of an overseas-headquartered group. Whether these entities are required to have any individuals approved as SMF7 is assessed on a case-by-case basis. Relevant considerations are likely to include:

- the respective organisational structures of the group and the relevant firm;
- the split of key responsibilities between the group and the UK boards and senior management; and
- whether SMFs based in the UK have an appropriate level of delegated authority from the group or parent to ensure that the UK entities comply with local regulatory obligations.

Non-executive Directors (NEDs)

As explained further in chapter 5, the Regulator has drawn a distinction between (i) NEDs who occupy the following roles: Chairman, Senior Independent Director or Committee Chairs (Non-notified or in-scope NEDS); and (ii) all other NEDs (Notified NEDs). Notified NEDs will not be Senior Managers, but will nevertheless be required to comply with Conduct Rules 1–5 (inclusive) and Senior Manager Conduct Rule 4.

Prescribed Responsibilities

Certain fundamental responsibilities are inherently contained within the definitions of each respective SMF. For example, the Chief Finance function (SMF2) is defined as *"the function responsible for the management of the financial resources of a firm and reporting to the management body of a firm in relation to its financial affairs"*.

In addition to these inherent responsibilities, the Regulator has designated 30 Prescribed Responsibilities for banking institutions. All applicable/relevant Prescribed Responsibilities must be assigned to those individuals who hold SMFs (except SMF18). Some responsibilities have been assigned to executives, while others are designed to reflect roles performed by NEDs.

The Regulator expects firms to allocate each Prescribed Responsibility to the most relevant Senior Manager. For instance, while firms will be able to assign responsibility for *"safeguarding the independence of the Head of Internal Audit function"* to any non-executive Senior Manager, the Regulator will typically expect this responsibility to be assigned to the Chair of the Audit Committee or the Chairman.

As with the list of SMFs, not all Prescribed Responsibilities will be relevant to all firms. The table below contains the full list of Prescribed Responsibilities; the *italicised* entries reflect those responsibilities to be allocated to NEDs.

All firms:

	Prescribed Responsibilities
1	Responsibility for the firm's performance of its obligations under the SMR
2	Responsibility for the firm's performance of its obligations under the employee certification regime
3	Responsibility for compliance with the requirements of the regulatory system about the management responsibilities map
4	Overall responsibility for the firm's policies and procedures for countering the risk that the firm might be used to further financial crime
5	Responsibility for the allocation of all prescribed responsibilities

Larger firms (firms with assets of more than £250m):

6	*Responsibility for: (a) leading the development of; and (b) monitoring the effective implementation of; policies and procedures for the induction, training and professional development of all members of the firm's governing body*
7	Responsibility for monitoring the effective implementation of policies and procedures for the induction, training and professional development of all persons performing designated senior management functions on behalf of the firm other than members of the governing body
8	Responsibility for overseeing the adoption of the firm's culture in the day-to-day management of the firm
9	*Responsibility for leading the development of the firm's culture by the governing body as a whole*
10	*Responsibility for: (a) safeguarding the independence of; and (b) oversight of the performance of; the internal audit function, in accordance with SYSC 6.2*
11	*Responsibility for: (a) safeguarding the independence of; and (b) oversight of the performance of; the compliance function, in accordance with SYSC 6.1*
12	*Responsibility for: (a) safeguarding the independence of; and (b) oversight of the performance of; the risk function, in accordance with SYSC 7.2.21R and SYSC 7.1.22R*
13	*Responsibility for overseeing the development, and implementation, of the firm's remuneration policies and practices, in accordance with SYSC 19D*
14	Responsibility for the independence, autonomy and effectiveness of the firm's policies and procedures on whistleblowing, including the procedures for protection of staff who raise concerns from detrimental treatment
15	Management of the allocation and maintenance of capital, funding and liquidity
16	The firm's treasury management functions

17	The production and integrity of the firm's financial information and its regulatory reporting in respect of its regulated activities
18	The firm's recovery plan and resolution pack and overseeing the internal processes regarding their governance
19	Responsibility for managing the firm's internal stress-tests and ensuring the accuracy and timeliness of information provided to the PRA and other regulatory bodies for the purposes of stress-testing
20	Responsibility for the development and maintenance of the firm's business model by the governing body
21	Responsibility for the firm's performance of its obligations under Fitness and Propriety in respect of its Notified NEDs

Applying in specified circumstances:

22	If the firm carries out proprietary trading, responsibility for the firm's proprietary trading activities
23	If the firm does not have an individual performing the Chief Risk function, overseeing and demonstrating that the risk management policies and procedures which the firm has adopted in accordance with SYSC 7.1.2R to SYSC 7.1.5R satisfy the requirements of those rules and are consistently effective in accordance with SYSC 4.1.1R
24	If the firm outsources its internal audit function, taking reasonable steps to ensure that every person involved in the performance of the service is independent from the persons who perform external audit, including: (a) supervision and management of the work of outsourced internal auditors; and (b) management of potential conflicts of interest between the provision of external audit and internal audit services
25	If the firm is a ring-fenced body, responsibility for ensuring that those aspects of the firm's affairs for which the person is responsible for managing are in compliance with the ring-fencing requirements
26	Overall responsibility for the firm's compliance with CASS

Small firms only (firms with assets of £250m or less):

27	Responsibility for implementing and management of the firm's risk management policies and procedures
28	Responsibility for managing the systems and controls of the firm
29	Responsibility for managing the firm's financial resources
30	Responsibility for ensuring the governing body is informed of its legal and regulatory obligations

It is anticipated that an appropriately abbreviated set of Prescribed Responsibilities will apply to non-banking institutions when the SMR is rolled out in 2018.

Other individuals with 'overall responsibility'

Those individuals with 'overall responsibility' for activities, functions or areas of the business need to be pre-approved as Senior Managers. In some cases, the individual who has overall responsibility for an activity, function or area will already have been identified as performing a specific SMF. However, it is essential that firms also identify any other individuals who have overall responsibility for an activity, function or area. Overall responsibility in this context means 'ultimate responsibility', under the firm's governing body, for managing or supervising a function, with direct responsibility for reporting to the governing body and putting matters for decision to it.

If an individual who has overall responsibility for an activity, function or area does not already hold any SMF, that person will need to be approved for SMF18.

3

PERSONAL REGULATORY LIABILITY

Introduction

This chapter addresses the channels through which the Regulator can pursue Senior Managers for failing to discharge their regulatory responsibilities.[8]

Sanctions available to the Regulator

An established failure by a Senior Manager to discharge their regulatory responsibilities can result in one or more of the following sanctions:

- imposition of a financial penalty of such amount as deemed appropriate;
- suspension, for an appropriate period, of 'approved person' status;
- variation of approval, through imposition of conditions;
- withdrawal of approval, if no longer deemed fit and proper;
- prohibition order, if not deemed fit and proper; and
- public censure.

These, in turn, will likely result in attendant reputational/career damage, as well as, potentially, personal bankruptcy.

Link to Fitness and Propriety

It does not follow that a Senior Manager found guilty of misconduct will necessarily fail to satisfy the 'fit and proper' requirements. However, any firm employing a Senior Manager who is found to be guilty of misconduct would be well advised to actively consider (and be seen to have considered) whether such individual remains fit and proper, notwithstanding their breach. In so doing, the firm would be expected to take into account the nature and extent of

---

[8]   Market abuse scenarios excepted, for present purposes.

the transgression – for example, whether a lack of probity or some 'lesser' form of misconduct was involved. Where a firm concludes that the individual does remain fit and proper, a record should be made of the basis of that determination. The firm might also prudently assume that the Regulator will pose the fit and proper question; and should therefore ensure that it can evidence that this issue was actively considered and the basis of the conclusion reached.

Avenues of personal regulatory exposure

There are a number of ways in which the Regulator can (separately or in combination) pursue a Senior Manager under the regulatory system[9] – namely, where the Senior Manager concerned:

(i) can be shown (by the Regulator) to have been 'knowingly concerned' in a contravention of a relevant regulatory requirement by the firm;

(ii) can be shown (by the Regulator) to have been personally culpable in respect of a breach of any of the Conduct Rules (including Senior Manager Conduct Rules (SM1–4)); or

(iii) can be shown (by the Regulator) to have breached the Duty of Responsibility – in other words, failed to take reasonable steps to avoid a regulatory contravention occurring (or continuing) within his or her area of responsibility.

In theory (at least), a Senior Manager within a banking institution could also be criminally liable under the new offence relating to a decision causing the financial institution to fail.[10]

In practical terms, it remains to be seen to what extent (if at all) the Duty of Responsibility is considered by the Regulator to differ substantially from Senior Manager Conduct Rule 2 (SM2)[11] – whether in technical terms or relative ease of enforcement.

---

[9]   Ignoring market abuse/misconduct offences, for present purposes.
[10]   Under section 36 of the Financial Services (Banking Reform) Act 2013.
[11]   Which requires Senior Managers to take reasonable steps to ensure that the business of the firm for which they are responsible complies with the relevant requirements and standards of the regulatory system.

In reality, the (Senior Manager) Conduct Rules and the Duty of Responsibility represent the two most likely avenues of potential exposure for Senior Managers.

The Regulator can opt to pursue a Senior Manager under either **or both** of these routes, in any given case.

Any case brought against a Senior Manager in these ways must be brought within **six years** of the Regulator becoming aware[12] of the alleged misconduct.[13]

As illustrated in chapters 4 and 5, **whichever route is pursued by the Regulator**, it will be important for Senior Managers to be able to demonstrate that they took reasonable steps/behaved reasonably in the particular circumstances. In other words, the risk mitigation measures to be employed are essentially the same, irrespective of whether the Regulator is alleging a breach of the (Senior Manager) Conduct Rules or the Duty of Responsibility.

Indeed, the regulator had explicitly acknowledged this inter-linkage:

"Senior Managers should be aware that one important consideration to which the FCA would expect to have regard, when determining whether or not a Senior Manager has complied with the duty [of responsibility], is whether the Senior Manager acted in accordance with their statutory, common law and other legal obligations, including, but not limited to, the Conduct Rules (and other relevant rules) set out in the FCA hand-book. There is considerable guidance on the reasonable steps a Senior Manager must take in the Conduct Rules. Senior Managers might find it helpful to have regard to the guidance on the duty when considering how to comply with the Conduct Rules."[14]

(Senior Manager) Conduct Rules

Senior Managers must observe (and continue to observe while remaining in post) each of the following Conduct Rules:

---

[12] The Regulator is to be treated as knowing of misconduct if it has information from which the misconduct can reasonably be inferred.
[13] Although this time-frame could be longer if the Senior Manager concerned has been served with a Warning Notice prior to the end of this period.
[14] Paragraph 2.6, CP 16/26.

Rule 1: You must act with integrity.

Rule 2: You must act with due skill, care and diligence.

Rule 3: You must be open and cooperative with the FCA, the PRA and other regulators.

Rule 4: You must pay due regard to the interests of customers and treat them fairly.

Rule 5: You must observe proper standards of market conduct.

Senior Manager Rule 1 (SC1): You must take reasonable steps to ensure that the business of the firm for which you are responsible is controlled effectively.

SC2: You must take reasonable steps to ensure that the business of the firm for which you are responsible complies with the relevant requirements and standards of the regulatory system.

SC3: You must take reasonable steps to ensure that any delegation of your responsibilities is to an appropriate person and that you oversee the discharge of the delegated responsibility effectively.

SC4: You must disclose appropriately any information of which the FCA or PRA would reasonably expect notice.

These Rules are very similar to the equivalent APER Statements of Principle, to which SIF holders were subject under the previous 'approved person' regime. The key differences are the introduction of new rules relating to: (i) customers' interests; and (ii) delegation.[15]

On one view,[16] Senior Managers may be particularly vulnerable under SC3 – given that most will necessarily have to delegate certain tasks/projects/issues. Specifically, a delegating Senior Manager is vulnerable to an allegation of ineffective oversight if, say, a regulatory contravention occurred under the 'watch' of the delegate. It would be open to the Regulator to argue that the Senior Manager cannot have taken the requisite reasonable steps to effectively oversee the delegate – otherwise, the contravention would simply not have

---

[15] Both of which were previously guidance/expectation, but have now been elevated to the status of a 'rule'.
[16] And not to diminish the importance of all other (Senior Manager) Conduct Rules.

occurred. As discussed later, it will be important for a Senior Manager facing such an allegation to be able to point to a good 'audit trail', evidencing the extent of delegate oversight.

A similar argument can also be made in respect of a Senior Manager's exposure under SC1 and SC2 – whereby the Regulator essentially infers that a relevant issue or breach would/could not have occurred if the Senior Manager had taken the requisite reasonable steps and that therefore, by deduction, he or she breached the relevant (Senior Manager) Conduct Rule. As discussed later, in any such situation the Senior Manager is essentially having to disprove the Regulator's contention – an effective reversal of the burden of proof.

Enforcement considerations

The Regulator may bring an enforcement action against a Senior Manager (in their capacity as such) based upon a suspected breach by that individual of one (or more) of the (Senior Manager) Conduct Rules. However, a Senior Manager will only be liable in this way where the Regulator can establish – on the balance of probabilities – that he or she is **personally culpable**.

When deciding whether to take action against an individual, the Regulator will take into account a number of considerations, including (but not limited to):

- the individual's position and responsibilities. The more senior the individual alleged to be responsible for the misconduct, the more seriously the Regulator is likely to view the misconduct, and therefore the more likely it is to take action against that individual;
- whether disciplinary action against the firm rather than the individual would be a more appropriate regulatory response;
- whether disciplinary action would be a proportionate response to the nature and seriousness of the breach by the individual;
- the nature, seriousness and impact of the suspected breach, including:
  - whether the breach was deliberate or reckless;
  - the duration and frequency of the breach;

- whether there are a number of smaller issues which individually may not justify disciplinary action, but do so when taken collectively; and
- the loss or risk of loss caused to consumers or other market users;
- the conduct of the individual after the alleged breach, including:
  - how quickly, effectively and completely the individual brought the breach to the attention of the Regulator;
  - the degree of cooperation the individual showed during the investigation of the breach; and
  - any remedial steps the individual has taken in respect of the breach; and
- the individual's previous disciplinary record and compliance history.

Accordingly, a suspected breach of a Senior Manager's responsibilities **may** – but not necessarily will – lead to a regulatory enforcement action against that individual.

Personal culpability

Personal culpability arises either where:

(i) the individual's behaviour was deliberate; or

(ii) their standard of conduct was below that which would be reasonable in all the circumstances at the time of the conduct concerned.

In determining whether or not a Senior Manager's conduct was 'reasonable in all the circumstances', the Regulator will take into account (among other things):

- whether the individual exercised reasonable care when considering relevant available information;
- whether he or she reached a reasonable conclusion on which he or she acted;
- the knowledge the individual had, or should have had, of regulatory concerns, if any, arising in the business under their control;
- the nature, scale and complexity of the business under management; and

- the specific role and responsibility of the individual concerned.

Therefore, a regulatory action will not necessarily be pursued against a Senior Manager simply because a regulatory failure has occurred in an area of business for which he or she is responsible. The Regulator will consider such action only where the Senior Manager's conduct was perceived to be either deliberate or below the standard which would be reasonable in all the circumstances at the time of the conduct concerned. This latter limb is an objective test which – it should be noted – is not necessarily referenced to the defendant's state of mind at the relevant time. In other words, an individual's conduct could be held to have been unreasonable in the circumstances, notwithstanding that he or she may at the relevant time have had the very best of intentions.

In reality, the majority of enforcement cases brought under the (Senior Manager) Conduct Rules by the Regulator against Senior Managers are therefore likely to hinge on the following key issue:

whether or not the Senior Manager's conduct was reasonable in all the circumstances.

'Reasonableness' is, however, an inherently vague concept; and is likely to be assessed by the Regulator, applying hindsight judgement. In practice, any allegation of personal culpability will often prove difficult for an individual to refute, absent a good argument (supported by evidence) that the Senior Manager took such measures as could reasonably have been expected in the particular circumstances.

On a practical level, therefore, prudent Senior Managers will routinely be considering what further measures they could reasonably be expected to take in the particular circumstances. Or, put another way, they will be asking 'what could I legitimately be criticised for not having done in the circumstances?'

Ideally, this thought process would (where appropriate) be accompanied by a documentary record of the measures taken (including any assurances received) and the basis upon which any ultimate decisions were made or courses of actions pursued.

Chapters 4 and 5 elaborate on this theme and offer some practical guidance and food for thought for Senior Managers.

Duty of Responsibility

Under the Duty of Responsibility, a Senior Manager will be guilty of misconduct where the Regulator can establish that:

(i) there has been, or continues to be, a breach of a relevant requirement[17] by the Senior Manager's firm; and

(ii) at the time of the contravention, the Senior Manager was responsible for the management of any of the firm's activities in relation to which the contravention occurred; and

(iii) he or she failed to take such steps as a person in that position could reasonably be expected to take to prevent the contravention occurring (or continuing) – an objective test.

The fact that the Regulator might previously have made findings and reached a bilateral settlement with a firm in relation to some or all of its breaches does not, however, mean that limb (i) is automatically satisfied.

As regards limb (ii), this will be a question of fact – in relation to which the individual's Statement of Responsibilities and the firm's Responsibility Map are likely to be important considerations. Other relevant considerations will include:

- how the firm operated, and how responsibilities were allocated in the firm, in practice;

- the Senior Manager's **actual** role and responsibilities in the firm – to be determined by reference to, amongst other things, the minutes of meetings, emails, interviews, telephone recordings and organisational charts; and

- the relationship between the Senior Manager's responsibilities and the responsibilities of other Senior Managers in the firm.

It has been indicated[18] that there will be no need for the Regulator to establish personal culpability when pursuing an individual under the Duty of Responsibility – a point which the Regulator emphasised in the wake of the abandonment of the controversial presumption of

---

[17] A requirement imposed by or under the FSMA, or by any qualifying EU provision specified by Treasury order.

[18] By Andrew Bailey (PRA) attending the Treasury Committee on 20 October 2015.

responsibility. However, given that the Regulator will still need to prove a failure to take reasonable steps, it is far from clear whether there is in fact any substantive difference (as compared with the scenario where the Regulator has to prove personal culpability for breach of the (Senior Manager) Conduct Rules). As discussed above,[19] personal culpability arises where an individual's conduct was deliberate or their standard of conduct was not reasonable in the circumstances.

Interestingly, the Regulator has confirmed that one important consideration to which it would have regard when determining whether or not a Senior Manager has complied with the Duty of Responsibility is whether the Senior Manager acted in accordance with the Conduct Rules. This could be taken to support the contention that there is little (if any) real practical distinction – in terms of relative ease of enforcement – between a case brought for breach of the Conduct Rules and one premised on a breach of the Duty of Responsibility.[20]

On this basis, it is certainly questionable whether the Regulator is in fact in any materially better position when pursuing an individual under the Duty of Responsibility.

Depending on the nature and extent of the firm's breach, and the scope of the individual Senior Manager's responsibilities, it is possible that more than one Senior Manager could be responsible. In such circumstances, the Regulator will consider whether it is appropriate to consider sanctioning one, some or all such Senior Managers.

There is no distinction made in the FSMA between executive and in-scope non-executive Senior Managers in relation to the Duty of Responsibility. However, it should be noted that the Regulator's ability to enforce under the Duty of Responsibility hinges on the scope of the responsibility in the first place – which for NEDs will typically be more limited[21] than for executive roles.

---

[19] See 'Personal culpability' section under 'Breach of (Senior Manager) Conduct Rules' above.

[20] Furthermore, the Regulator has effectively acknowledged the inter-linkage between the 'reasonable steps' guidance provided, respectively, in the context of: (i) the Conduct Rules; and (ii) the Duty of Responsibility (paragraph 2.6, CP 16/26).

[21] As should be duly reflected in a NED's Statement of Responsibilities.

Collective decisions

Senior Managers are, in principle, accountable for their individual contributions to collective decisions and their implementation insofar as they concern any of the firm's activities for which they are responsible. Indeed, the Regulator has confirmed its view that the SMR is consistent with, and complementary to, the principle of collective decision-making. What, if any, appetite the Regulator has for pursuing a Senior Manager directly in respect of a collective decision in which he or she participated remains to be seen.

Reasonable Steps Defence

In determining whether a Senior Manager has taken the necessary 'reasonable steps' in any given situation, the Regulator will consider the full circumstances of each case and assess: (i) the steps the Senior Manager actually took; against (ii) such steps as the Regulator considers that a Senior Manager in that position could reasonably have been expected to take. The Regulator's expectations of the steps in (ii) will necessarily depend on the individual circumstances as they existed at the time. *"It is not the [Regulator's] intention to apply standards 'retrospectively' or with the benefit of hindsight."*[22]

Such steps as a person in the position of the Senior Manager could reasonably be expected to take to avoid the firm's contravention of a relevant requirement occurring (or continuing) are:

(i) such steps as a competent Senior Manager would have taken;

(ii) at that time;

(iii) in that specific individual's position;

(iv) with that individual's role and responsibilities; and

(v) in all the existing circumstances.

When determining whether or not a Senior Manager took the requisite reasonable steps, additional considerations to which the Regulator is likely to have regard include (but are not limited to):

---

[22] Paragraph 2.74, SS28/15, July 2015.

- the role and responsibilities of the Senior Manager (primarily by reference to his or her Statement of Responsibilities);
- whether the Senior Manager exercised reasonable care when considering available information;
- whether the Senior Manager reached a reasonable conclusion on which to act;
- the nature, scale and complexity of the firm's business;
- the knowledge the Senior Manager had, or should have had (taking into account, among other factors, the length of time he or she had been in the role and handover arrangements to those new in a role), of regulatory concerns, if any, relating to their role and responsibilities;
- what expertise and competence the Senior Manager had, or ought to have, possessed at the time to perform his or her specific Senior Manager function;
- whether the Senior Manager, where he or she was, or should have been, aware of actual or suspected issues that involved possible breaches by the firm of relevant requirements relating to his or her role and responsibilities, took reasonable steps to ensure that they were dealt with in a timely and appropriate manner;
- what steps the Senior Manager could have taken, considering what alternative actions might have been open to the Senior Manager at the time and the timeliness within which he or she could have acted;
- whether the Senior Manager acted in accordance with their statutory, common law and other legal obligations, including, but not limited to, the (Senior Manager) Conduct Rules (and other relevant rules) set out in the FCA Handbook,[23] those set out in the Companies Act 2006,[24] the Regulator's handbook and, if the firm was listed on the London Stock Exchange, the UK Corporate Governance Code and related guidance;

---

[23] Which factor would appear to support the questionable practical distinction between SC2 and the Duty of Responsibility.

[24] Though it is questionable how this will operate in practice, given that statutory duties and regulatory responsibilities are aimed at protecting the interests of different stakeholder groups (broadly, shareholders and clients, respectively). Chapter 8 considers this subject in more detail.

- whether the Senior Manager took reasonable steps to ensure that any delegation of his or her responsibilities, where this was itself reasonable, was to an appropriate person, with the necessary capacity, competence, knowledge, seniority or skill; and whether the Senior Manager took reasonable steps to oversee and monitor the discharge of the delegated responsibility effectively;

- whether the Senior Manager took reasonable steps to ensure that the reporting lines, whether in the UK or overseas, in relation to the firm's activities for which he or she was responsible, were clear to staff and operated effectively;

- whether the Senior Manager took reasonable steps to satisfy themselves, on reasonable grounds, that, for the activities for which they were responsible, the firm had appropriate policies and procedures for reviewing the competence, knowledge, skills and performance of each individual member of staff, to assess their suitability to fulfil their duties;

- whether the Senior Manager took reasonable steps to assess, on taking up each of their responsibilities, and monitor, where reasonable, the governance, operational and risk management arrangements in place for the firm's activities for which the Senior Manager was responsible (including, where appropriate, corroborating, challenging and considering the wider implications of the information available), and whether he or she took reasonable steps to deal with any actual or suspected issues identified as a result in a timely and appropriate manner;

- the actual responsibilities of that Senior Manager and the relationship between those responsibilities and those of other Senior Managers in the firm (including in relation to any joint responsibilities or matrix management structures);

- whether the Senior Manager took reasonable steps to ensure an orderly transition when another Senior Manager under his or her oversight or responsibility was replaced in the performance of that function by someone else;

- whether the Senior Manager took reasonable steps to ensure an orderly transition when being replaced in the performance of his or her function by someone else;

- whether the Senior Manager took reasonable steps to understand and inform themselves about the firm's activities in relation to which they were responsible, including, but not limited to, whether they:
  - permitted the expansion or restructuring of the business without reasonably assessing the potential risks;
  - inadequately monitored highly profitable transactions, business practices, unusual transactions or individuals who contributed significantly to the profitability of a business area or who had significant influence over the operation of a business area;
  - failed to obtain independent expert opinion, where appropriate from within or outside the firm, as appropriate;
  - failed to ensure adequate reporting or seek an adequate explanation of issues within a business area, whether from people within that business area, or elsewhere within or outside the firm if they were not an expert in that area;
  - failed to maintain an appropriate level of understanding about an issue or responsibility that they delegated to an individual or individuals;
- whether the Senior Manager took reasonable steps to ensure that, where involved in a collective decision affecting the firm's activities for which he or she was responsible, where it was reasonable for the decision to be taken collectively, he or she informed himself/ herself of the relevant matters before taking part in the decision, and exercised reasonable care, skill and diligence in contributing to it;
- whether the Senior Manager took reasonable steps to follow the firm's procedures, where this was itself appropriate;
- the overall circumstances and environment at the firm and more widely in which such a Senior Manager was operating at the time. For example, the Regulator may consider whether the way in which he or she prioritised matters was informed by an appropriate risk assessment and how he or she responded to new developments;

- how long the Senior Manager had been in role, with their responsibilities, and whether there was an orderly transition and handover when they took up the role and responsibilities; and
- whether the Senior Manager took reasonable steps to implement (either personally or through a compliance department or other departments) adequate and appropriate systems and controls to comply with the relevant requirements and standards of the regulatory system for the activities of the firm.

In relation to the steps that a Senior Manager actually took to avoid the contravention occurring (or continuing), examples of steps that may be considered relevant, depending on the circumstances, might include:

- pre-emptive actions to prevent a breach occurring, including initial reviews of the business on taking up a Senior Manager function;[25]
- implementing, policing and reviewing appropriate policies and procedures;
- awareness of relevant requirements and standards of the regulatory system;
- investigations or reviews of the Senior Manager's area of responsibility;
- where a breach is continuing, the response to that breach;
- structuring and control of day-to-day operations, including ensuring that any delegations are managed and reviewed appropriately (including in relation to any matrix management arrangements);
- obtaining appropriate internal management information, and critically interrogating and monitoring that information;
- raising issues, reviewing issues and following them up with relevant staff, committees and boards;
- seeking and obtaining appropriate expert advice or assurance, whether internal or external;
- ensuring the firm and/or relevant area(s) have adequate resources, and that these are appropriately deployed, including for risk and control functions; and

---

[25] See the discussion of the *Pottage* case in chapter 4.

- awareness of relevant external developments, including key risks.

Evidence that the Regulator might seek to obtain in respect of these kinds of matters might include:

- board and committee minutes;
- minutes of other internal meetings;
- Statements of Responsibilities and Responsibilities Maps;
- organisation charts and information on reporting lines;
- any other internal materials – for example, emails or telephone recordings; and
- regulatory correspondence and interviews.

Chapters 4 and 5 consider these indicators in further detail, and offer some practical risk management guidance for Senior Managers.

Competing priorities

The Regulator has consciously veered away from providing 'reasonable steps' guidance on the management of competing priorities: *"We do not believe that it would be helpful ... and want to avoid giving the impression that Senior Managers would not be guilty of misconduct merely by demonstrating that they were faced with competing priorities, or that it is acceptable for a busy Senior Manager to deprioritise concerns about conduct."*[26]

---

[26] Paragraph 2.15, CP 16/26.

4

MANAGING REGULATORY EXPOSURE

INTRODUCTION

Section A of this chapter (which includes regulatory expectations of Senior Managers and managing personal regulatory exposure) is relevant to all Senior Managers holding executive roles – irrespective of their particular function. Section B serves as an effective overlay for those occupying Chief Executive Office (CEO), executive director, non-executive director and compliance oversight functions.

Senior Managers holding non-executive roles can skip section A of this chapter; and focus on the relevant parts of section B and the whole of chapter 5.

This chapter elaborates upon those issues discussed in chapter 3.

A. GENERAL

1. Regulatory expectations of Senior Managers

The table below consolidates PRA (*see* blue *text*) and joint PRA and FCA (*see* green *text*) expectations of Senior Managers under the SMR.

There follow some key questions for Senior Managers to consider in addressing these regulatory expectations, alongside some accompanying insight and commentary.

PRA AND FCA PRONOUNCEMENTS

The SMR's emphasis on individual responsibilities is not, however, intended to undermine the fiduciary, legal and regulatory responsibilities of the board which will retain ultimate decision-making power and authority over all aspects of the firm's affairs.[27]

The role of a board sub-committee is to support the board. The committees are accountable to the board, but should not relieve the board of any of its responsibilities.[28]

Regulatory expectations

An effective board is one which understands the business, establishes a clear strategy, articulates a clear risk appetite to support that strategy, oversees an effective risk control framework, and collectively has the skills, the experience and the confidence to hold executive management rigorously to account for delivering that strategy and managing within that risk appetite.[29]

... the PRA expects the boards and management of regulated firms to run the business prudently, consistent with the firm's own safety and soundness and the continuing stability of the financial system.

---

[27] Joint PRA and FCA, paragraph 2.6 of FCA CP14/13 / PRA CP14/14, "Strengthening Accountability in Banking: A New Regulatory Framework for Individuals", July 2014.

[28] PRA, paragraph 13.1 of the Appendix to CP18/15, "Corporate Governance: Board Responsibilities", May 2015

[29] PRA, paragraph 1.3 of CP18/15, "Corporate Governance: Board Responsibilities", May 2015.

The desired outcome from a regulatory standpoint is an effective board, which is one that:

- establishes a sustainable business model and a clear strategy consistent with that model;
- articulates and oversees a clear and measurable statement of risk appetite against which major business options are actively assessed; and
- meets its regulatory obligations, is open with the regulators and sets a culture that supports prudent management. [30]

KEY QUESTIONS TO CONSIDER

Regulatory expectations

Questions

Could I credibly articulate:

- my firm's stated strategy?
- the firm's risk appetite supporting that strategy?
- the firm's risk control framework?
- the key regulatory and operational risks faced by my firm?
- my firm's espoused cultural expectations?

Comments

The relationship between the board and Senior Managers

One of the key aims of the SMR is to ensure that Senior Managers are individually accountable for those areas over which they have been designated responsibility.

The fact that certain Senior Managers will not be members of the board does not serve to absolve the board of its collective duties/ responsibilities. The Regulator has clarified that the board will retain ultimate decision-making power and authority over all aspects of

---

[30] PRA, paragraph 1.2 of the Appendix to CP18/15, "Corporate Governance: Board Responsibilities", May 2015.

the firm's affairs, and that the SMR is not intended to undermine the fiduciary, legal and regulatory responsibilities of the board.

The Regulator's broader expectations of Senior Managers

Questions

- Does the board/committee meet with sufficient frequency and duration to allow for effective oversight and discussion?
- Is the management information provided to me sufficiently informative? Is it unwieldy and unfathomable? Is it provided in good time to enable me to properly digest?
- Am I confident that I have access to all relevant management information and external information to ensure that I am fully appraised? Do I have any sense that certain potentially relevant information is being withheld?

Comments

The Regulator is now commonly requiring sight of board/committee papers and minutes, as well as periodically requesting to attend and observe such meetings in person.

The Regulator will also likely focus on a number of key cultural indicators, and evidence that customers' interests really are being put at the forefront of consideration and afforded due weight.

Senior Managers should also keep (or be kept) abreast of relevant regulatory developments, and should have a good general appreciation of the regulatory environment in which their firm is operating.

Without sufficiently informative management information, Senior Managers will not be properly equipped to perform their role. However, overly granular and unwieldy management information can prove to be counter-productive, and has been seen to attract regulatory criticism. Therefore, a sensible balance must be struck in practice. The board/committee secretariat should be constructively responsive to any suggestions in this regard.

2. Determining a Senior Manager's scope of responsibility

The table below consolidates the relevant PRA (*see* blue *text*) and FCA (*see* red *text*) provisions in relation to the determination of a Senior Manager's scope of responsibility. The table is followed by some key questions for Senior Managers to address; alongside some accompanying insights and commentary.

PRA AND FCA PRONOUNCEMENTS

Whether a Senior Manager is or is not responsible for managing any of the firm's relevant activities will be a question of fact. Statements of Responsibility and Responsibilities Maps should be relevant evidence but the PRA may look beyond these if it considers it appropriate. [ii]

Firms may wish to allocate to a Senior Manager responsibilities not covered in the PRA's or FCA's rules. The PRA may also require a firm to allocate responsibility for a given regulatory deliverable not covered elsewhere in its rules to a specific Senior Manager.

An SMF manager may carry out responsibilities (as described in the statement of responsibilities) which go beyond applicable prescribed requirements, or a firm may include additional information about such prescribed requirements with the statement of responsibilities. However, any additional responsibilities or additional information should not reduce, alter the scope of, dilute or undermine the prescribed requirements. [iv]

Firms are required to ensure that one or more SMFs have overall responsibility for each of the activities, business areas and management functions of the firm ... Once they have identified staff holding prescribed responsibilities, firms have the flexibility to allocate overall responsibility for other aspects of their business to

---

[31] PRA, paragraph 2.71 of Supervisory Statement SS28/15, "Strengthening Individual Accountability in Banking", July 2015.

[32] PRA, paragraph 2.32 of FCA CP14/13 / PRA CP14/14, "Strengthening Accountability in Banking: A New Regulatory Framework for Individuals", July 2014 ; handbook text SUP 10C.11.26G(4): CP15/22, "Strengthening Accountability in Banking: Final Rules (Including Feedback on CP14/31 and CP 15/5) and Consultation on Extending the Certification Regime to Wholesale Market Activities", July 2015.

their senior managers as they see fit, ensuring that there are no gaps.[33]

SoRs are required to detail exactly what each Senior Manager is responsible for. They are intended to drive benefits through requiring firms to properly consider their arrangements and 'who does what'. They also underpin the presumption of responsibility by clearly delineating who is presumed to be responsible for what.[34]

When SYSC 4.7 refers to a person having overall responsibility for a function, it means a person who has:

(1) ultimate responsibility (under the governing body) for managing or supervising that function; and

(2) primary and direct responsibility for:

(a) briefing and reporting to the governing body about that function; and

(b) putting matters for decision about that function to the governing body.

Having overall responsibility for a matter does not mean having ultimate authority over it. The ultimate decision-making body of a firm is its governing body, acting collectively.[35]

When determining, for the purposes of section 66A(5) of the Act, whether an SMF manager was responsible for the management of any of the firm's activities in relation to which a contravention of a relevant requirement by the firm occurred, the FCA will consider the full circumstances of each case. A list of considerations that may be

---

[33] FCA, paragraph 2.10 of CP15/9, "Strengthening Accountability in Banking: A New Regulatory Framework for Individuals – Feedback on FCA CP14/13 / PRA CP14/14 and Consultation on Additional Guidance", March 2015; handbook text SYSC 4.7.8R: CP15/22, "Strengthening Accountability in Banking: Final Rules (Including Feedback on CP14/31 and CP 15/5) and Consultation on Extending the Certification Regime to wholesale market activities", July 2015.

[34] FCA, paragraph 2.12 of CP15/9, "Strengthening Accountability in Banking: A New Regulatory Framework for Individuals – Feedback on FCA CP14/13 / PRA CP14/14 and Consultation on Additional Guidance", March 2015.

[35] Handbook text SYSC 4.7.11 G and SYSC 4.7.12 G: CP15/22, "Strengthening Accountability in Banking: Final Rules (Including Feedback on CP14/31 and CP 15/5) and Consultation on Extending the Certification Regime to Wholesale Market Activities", July 2015.

relevant for this purpose is set out below. This list is not exhaustive: there may be other considerations, not listed, that are relevant.

(1) The SMF manager's statement of responsibilities, including whether the SMF manager was performing an executive or non-executive role.

(2) The firm's management responsibilities map.

(3) How the firm operated, and how responsibilities were allocated in the firm in practice.

(4) The SMF manager's actual role and responsibilities in the firm, to be determined by reference to, among other things, the minutes of meetings, emails, interviews, telephone recordings and organisational charts.

(5) The relationship between the SMF manager's responsibilities and the responsibilities of other SMF managers in the firm.[36]

KEY QUESTIONS TO CONSIDER

Questions

- Is my Statement of Responsibilities sufficiently clear and accurately reflective of what I signed up for? Are there any ambiguities that might usefully be clarified?

- Is the firm's Responsibilities Map consistent and reconcilable with my Statement of Responsibilities?

- Is my Statement of Responsibilities consistent with the terms of reference of the committees on which I sit?

- Are my Statement of Responsibilities and the Responsibilities Map consistent with the actual responsibilities I undertake in practice? In reality, am I also entrusted with, or have I assumed, certain de facto responsibilities which are not documented? Do board/committee minutes (to the extent applicable) appropriately

---

[36] Draft handbook text DEPP 6.2.9 CG: CP15/9, "Strengthening Accountability in Banking: A New Regulatory Framework for Individuals – Feedback on FCA CP14/13 / PRA CP14/14 and Consultation on Additional Guidance", March 2015.

reflect my responsibilities? Or might they, for example, present an impression that I am responsible for more than I have signed up to?

Comments

Considerations for Senior Managers

Senior Managers should review their Statements of Responsibility carefully to ensure that they are clear, unambiguous and reflective of the Senior Manager's agreed remit. Senior Managers should also check that their Statements of Responsibilities are entirely consistent with: (i) the terms of reference of any committees to which they belong; and (ii) the Responsibilities Map.

The Regulator will assess a Senior Manager's scope of responsibility by reference to all applicable circumstances. Whilst the Statement of Responsibilities and Responsibilities Map are clearly key considerations, **they will not be determinative where the practical reality is different**. In other words, the Regulator will look beyond the documentation to the actualities.

Senior Managers might therefore usefully review, periodically, whether their Statements of Responsibility continue to represent reality. Any perceived discrepancies should be raised and resolved, as lack of clarity is not in the interests of either the Senior Manager or the firm (and runs contrary to one of the underpinning principles of the SMR).

Senior Managers should also remain vigilant to ensure that they do not inadvertently assume any additional responsibilities to which they did not originally agree or sign up. For example, this may arise if a Senior Manager is asked to take on a particular oversight role, or where a Senior Manager voluntarily assumes additional responsibilities, which go beyond his or her formally agreed remit.

3. Managing personal regulatory exposure

There are a number of ways in which the Regulator can pursue a Senior Manager under the regulatory system[37] – namely, where the Senior Manager concerned:

(i) can be shown (by the Regulator) to have been 'knowingly concerned' in a contravention of a relevant regulatory requirement by the firm;

(ii) can be shown (by the Regulator) to have been personally culpable in respect of a breach of any of the Conduct Rules or Senior Manager Conduct Rules (SM1–4); or

(iii) can be shown (by the Regulator) to have breached the Duty of Responsibility – that is, by establishing that he or she failed to take reasonable steps to prevent the relevant contravention occurring (or continuing) within their area of responsibility.

As a practical matter (and as alluded to earlier), it remains to be seen to what extent (if at all) the Duty of Responsibility is considered by the Regulator to differ from SC2 – whether in technical terms or relative ease of enforcement.

A Senior Manager of a bank could also be criminally liable under the offence relating to a decision causing the financial institution to fail.[38]

The table below consolidates relevant PRA (*see* blue *text*) and FCA (*see* red *text*) rules/commentary/guidance relating to the Senior Manager Conduct Rules – (together with the Duty of Responsibility) the most likely avenue of potential exposure for Senior Managers, in practice. **Significantly, and irrespective of the precise route pursued by the Regulator, it will be important for Senior Managers to be able to demonstrate that they took reasonable steps/behaved reasonably in the particular circumstances**. The table also incorporates some pointers as to what may constitute 'reasonable steps', as referenced in the PRA's Supervisory Statement (SS28/15) and FCA Consultation Paper CP16/26.

---

[37] Ignoring market abuse/misconduct offences for the present purposes.
[38] Under section 36 of the Financial Services (Banking Reform) Act 2013.

The table is followed by some key questions for Senior Managers to consider in addressing regulatory requirements and expectations, and in helping to establish 'reasonable steps/behaviour', alongside some related commentary and insights.

PRA AND FCA PRONOUNCEMENTS

Senior Manager Conduct Rules (COCON 2.1, 2.2, 4.1 and 4.2)

Rule 2: You must act with due skill, care and diligence

Acting with due skill, etc as a manager

- It is important for a manager to understand the business for which they are responsible. A manager is unlikely to be an expert in all aspects of a complex financial services business. However, they should understand and inform themselves about the business sufficiently to understand the risks of its trading, credit or other business activities.

- It is important for a manager to understand the risks of expanding the business into new areas and, before approving the expansion, they should investigate and satisfy themselves, on reasonable grounds, about the risks, if any, to the business.

- Where unusually profitable business is undertaken, or where the profits are particularly volatile or the business involves funding requirements on the firm beyond those reasonably anticipated, a manager should require explanations from those who report to him. Where those explanations are implausible or unsatisfactory, they should take steps to test the veracity of those explanations.

- Where a manager is not an expert in a business area, they should consider whether they (or those with whom they work) have the necessary expertise to provide an adequate explanation of issues within that business area. If not, they should seek an independent opinion from elsewhere within or outside the firm.

The following is a non-exhaustive list of examples of conduct by a manager that would be in breach of rule 2.

(1) Failing to take reasonable steps to ensure that the business of the firm for which he has responsibility:

  (a) is controlled effectively;

  (b) complies with the relevant requirements and standards of the regulatory system applicable to that area of the business; and

  (c) is conducted in such a way to ensure that any delegation of responsibilities is to an appropriate person and is overseen effectively.

(2) Failing to take reasonable steps to adequately inform themselves about the affairs of the business for which they are responsible, including:

  (a) permitting transactions without a sufficient understanding of the risks involved;

  (b) permitting expansion of the business without reasonably assessing the potential risks of that expansion;

  (c) inadequately monitoring highly profitable transactions or business practices or unusual transactions or business practices;

  (d) accepting implausible or unsatisfactory explanations from subordinates without testing the veracity of those explanations; and

  (e) failing to obtain independent, expert opinion where appropriate.

(3) Failing to take reasonable steps to maintain an appropriate level of understanding about an issue or part of the business that the manager has delegated to an individual or individuals (whether in-house or outside contractors).

SC1: You must take reasonable steps to ensure that the business of the firm for which you are responsible is controlled effectively

• An SMF manager's role and responsibilities are set out in the statement of responsibilities.

- Strategy and plans will often dictate the risk which the business is prepared to take on and high level controls will dictate how the business is to be run. If the strategy of the business is to enter high-risk areas, then the degree of control and strength of monitoring reasonably required within the business will be high. In organising the business for which they are responsible, an SMF manager should bear this in mind.

- To comply with the obligations of rule SC1, an SMF manager may find it helpful to review whether each area of the business for which they are responsible has been clearly assigned to a particular individual or individuals.

- The organisation of the business and the responsibilities of those within it should be clearly defined. Reporting lines should be clear to staff. Where staff have dual reporting lines there is a greater need to ensure that the responsibility and accountability of each individual line manager is clearly set out and understood.

- Where members of staff have particular levels of authorisation, these should be clearly set out and communicated to staff. It may be appropriate for each member of staff to have a job description of which they are aware.

- An SMF manager should take reasonable steps to satisfy themselves, on reasonable grounds, that each area of the business for which they are responsible has appropriate policies and procedures for reviewing the competence, knowledge, skills and performance of each individual member of staff.

- If an individual's performance is unsatisfactory, then the relevant SMF manager should review carefully whether to allow that individual to continue in their position. In particular:

  (1) If they are aware of concerns relating to the compliance with requirements and standards of the regulatory system (or internal controls) of the individual concerned, or of staff reporting to that individual, the SMF manager should take care not to give undue weight to the financial performance of the individual or group concerned when considering whether any action should be taken.

(2) An adequate investigation of the concerns should be undertaken (including, where appropriate, adherence to internal controls). The SMF manager should be satisfied, on reasonable grounds, that the investigation is appropriate, the results are accurate and that the concerns do not pose an unacceptable risk to compliance with the requirements and standards of the regulatory system.

As part of organising the business, an SMF manager should ensure that there is an orderly transition when another SMF manager under their oversight or responsibility ceases to perform that function and someone else takes up that function. It would be appropriate for the individual vacating such a position to prepare a comprehensive set of handover notes for his successor. Those notes should, at a minimum, specify any matter that is ongoing which the successor would reasonably expect to be aware of to:

(1) perform their function effectively;

(2) ensure compliance with the requirements and standards of the regulatory system; and

(3) ensure that the individual with overall responsibility for that part of the business of the firm maintains effective control.

In organising the business, an SMF manager should pay attention to any temporary vacancies which exist. They should take reasonable steps to ensure that suitable cover for responsibilities is arranged. This could include taking on temporary staff or external consultants. The SMF manager should assess the risk that is posed to compliance with the requirements and standards of the regulatory system as a result of the vacancy, and the higher the risk the greater the steps they should take to fill the vacancy. It may be appropriate to limit or suspend the activity if adequate cover for responsibilities cannot be arranged. To the extent that those vacancies are for controlled functions, they may only be filled by persons approved for that function.

- The following is a non-exhaustive list of examples of conduct that would be in breach of rule SC1.

  (1) Failing to take reasonable steps to apportion responsibilities for all areas of the business under the approved person's control.

  (2) Failing to take reasonable steps to apportion responsibilities clearly among those to whom responsibilities have been delegated, which includes establishing confusing or uncertain:

  (a) reporting lines; or

  (b) authorisation levels; or

  (c) job descriptions and responsibilities.

  (3) In the case of a manager who is responsible for dealing with the apportionment of responsibilities, failing to take reasonable care to maintain a clear and appropriate apportionment of responsibilities, including:

  (a) failing to review regularly the responsibilities which have been apportioned; and

  (b) failing to act where that review shows that those responsibilities have not been clearly apportioned.

  (4) Failing to take reasonable steps to ensure that suitable individuals are responsible for those aspects of the business under the control of the individual performing a senior management function, including the following:

  (a) failing to review the competence, knowledge, skills and performance of staff to assess their suitability to fulfil their duties, despite evidence that their performance is unacceptable;

  (b) giving undue weight to financial performance when considering the suitability or continuing suitability of an individual for a particular role; and

  (c) allowing managerial vacancies which put compliance with the requirements and standards of the regulatory system at risk to remain, without arranging suitable cover for the responsibilities.

SC2: You must take reasonable steps to ensure that the business of the firm for which you are responsible complies with the relevant requirements and standards of the regulatory system

- An SMF manager must take reasonable steps both to ensure his firm's compliance with the relevant requirements and standards of the regulatory system and to ensure that all staff are aware of the need for compliance.

- An SMF manager need not themself put in place the systems of control for the business, unless it is within their role and responsibilities. However, they should take reasonable steps to ensure that the business for which they are responsible has operating procedures and systems with well-defined steps for complying with the detail of relevant requirements and standards of the regulatory system and for ensuring that the business is run prudently. The nature and extent of the systems of control that are required will depend upon the relevant requirements and standards of the regulatory system, and the nature, scale and complexity of the business.

- Where an SMF manager becomes aware of actual or suspected problems that involve possible breaches of relevant requirements and standards of the regulatory system falling within their area of responsibility, they should take reasonable steps to ensure that they are dealt with in a timely and appropriate manner. This may involve an adequate investigation to find out whether any systems or procedures have failed and why. They may need to obtain expert opinion on the adequacy and efficacy of the systems and procedures.

- If an issue raises questions of law or interpretation, an SMF manager may need to take legal advice. If appropriate legal expertise is not available in-house, they may need to consider appointing an appropriate external adviser.

- Where independent reviews of systems and procedures have been undertaken and result in recommendations for improvement, the SMF manager responsible for that business area should ensure that, unless there are good reasons not to, any reasonable recommendations are implemented in a timely manner. What is reasonable will depend on the nature of the issue to be addressed and the cost of the improvement. It will be reasonable for the SMF manager to carry out a cost benefit analysis when assessing whether the recommendations are reasonable.

- The following is a non-exhaustive list of examples of conduct that would be in breach of rule SC2.

  (1) Failing to take reasonable steps to implement (either personally or through a compliance department or other departments) adequate and appropriate systems of control to comply with the relevant requirements and standards of the regulatory system for the activities of the firm.

  (2) Failing to take reasonable steps to monitor (either personally or through a compliance department or other departments) compliance with the relevant requirements and standards of the regulatory system for the activities of the firm in question.

  (3) Failing to take reasonable steps to inform themselves adequately about the reason why significant breaches (suspected or actual) of the relevant requirements and standards of the regulatory system for the activities of the firm in question may have arisen (taking account of the systems and procedures in place). This would include failing to investigate whether systems or procedures may have failed and failing to obtain expert opinion on the adequacy of the systems and procedures where appropriate.

  (4) Failing to take reasonable steps to ensure that procedures and systems of control are reviewed and, if appropriate, improved, following the identification of significant breaches (suspected or actual) of the relevant requirements and

standards of the regulatory system relating to the activities of the firm including:

(a) unreasonably failing to implement recommendations for improvements in systems and procedures; and

(b) unreasonably failing to implement recommendations for improvements to systems and procedures in a timely manner.

(5) For a manager with responsibility for overseeing the establishment and maintenance of appropriate systems and controls or the apportionment of responsibilities, any failure to take reasonable care, to ensure that these obligations are discharged effectively.

(6) For a proprietary trader, failing to maintain and comply with appropriate systems and controls in relation to that activity.

(7) For a money laundering reporting officer, failing to discharge the responsibilities imposed on them by the firm for oversight of its compliance with the FCA's rules on systems and controls against money laundering.

(8) For an SMF manager who is responsible for the compliance function, failing to ensure that:

(a) the compliance function has the necessary authority, resources, expertise and access to all relevant information; or

(b) a compliance officer is appointed and is responsible for the compliance function and for any reporting as to compliance; or

(c) the persons involved in the compliance functions are not involved in the performance of services or activities they monitor; or

(d) the method of determining the remuneration of the persons involved in the compliance function does not compromise their objectivity; or

(e) the method of determining the remuneration complies, where applicable, with the Remuneration Code.

> *SC3: You must take reasonable steps to ensure that any delegation of your responsibilities is to an appropriate person and that you oversee the discharge of the delegated responsibility effectively*
>
> - An SMF manager may delegate the investigation, resolution or management of an issue or authority for dealing with a part of the business to individuals who report to them or to others.
>
> - An SMF manager should have reasonable grounds for believing that the delegate has the competence, knowledge, skill and time to deal with the issue. For instance, if the compliance department only has sufficient resources to deal with day-to-day issues, it would be unreasonable to delegate to it the resolution of a complex or unusual issue without ensuring it had sufficient capacity to deal with the matter adequately.
>
> - The FCA recognises that an SMF manager will have to exercise their own judgement in deciding how issues are dealt with and sometimes that judgement will, with the benefit of hindsight, be shown to have been wrong. The SMF manager will not be in breach of rule SC3 in COCON 2.2.3R unless they fail to exercise due and reasonable consideration before they delegate the resolution of an issue or authority for dealing with a part of the business and fail to reach a reasonable conclusion. If they are in doubt about how to deal with an issue or the seriousness of a particular compliance problem, then, although they cannot delegate to the FCA the responsibility for dealing with the problem or issue, they can speak to the FCA to discuss his approach.
>
> - An SMF manager will not always manage the business on a day-to-day basis themselves. The extent to which they do so will depend on a number of factors, including the nature, scale and complexity of the business and their position within it. The larger and more complex the business, the greater the need for clear and effective delegation and reporting lines, which may involve documenting the scope of that delegation and the reporting lines in writing. The FCA will look to the SMF manager to take reasonable steps to ensure that systems are in place to ensure

that issues are being addressed at the appropriate level. When issues come to their attention, they should deal with them in an appropriate way.

- Delegating the authority for dealing with an issue or a part of the business to an individual or individuals (whether in-house or outside contractors) without reasonable grounds for believing that the delegate had the necessary capacity, competence, knowledge, seniority or skill to deal with the issue or to take authority for dealing with part of the business indicates a failure to comply with rule SC3 in COCON 2.2.3R.

- Although an SMF manager may delegate the resolution of an issue, or authority for dealing with a part of the business, they cannot delegate responsibility for it. It is that person's responsibility to ensure that they receive reports on progress and question those reports where appropriate. For instance, if progress appears to be slow or if the issue is not being resolved satisfactorily, then the SMF manager may need to challenge the explanations they receive and, take action personally to resolve the problem. This may include increasing the resource applied to it, reassigning the resolution internally or obtaining external advice or assistance. Where an issue raises significant concerns, an SMF manager should act clearly and decisively. If appropriate, this may be by suspending members of staff or relieving them of all or part of their responsibilities.

- The following is a non-exhaustive list of examples of conduct that would be in breach of rule SC3.

  (1) Failing to take reasonable steps to maintain an appropriate level of understanding about an issue or part of the business that he has delegated to an individual(s) (whether in-house or outside contractors) including:

    (a) disregarding an issue or part of the business once it has been delegated;

    (b) failing to require adequate reports once the resolution of an issue or management of part of the business has been delegated; and

(c) accepting implausible or unsatisfactory explanations from delegates without testing their accuracy.

(2) Failing to supervise and monitor adequately the individual(s) (whether in-house or outside contractors) to whom responsibility for dealing with an issue or authority for dealing with a part of the business has been delegated including any failure to:

(a) take personal action where progress is unreasonably slow, or where implausible or unsatisfactory explanations are provided; or

(b) review the performance of an outside contractor in connection with the delegated issue or business.

- In determining whether or not the conduct of an SMF manager complies with rule SC3 in COCON 2.2.3R, the factors which the FCA would expect to take into account include:

(1) the competence, knowledge or seniority of the delegate; and

(2) the past performance and record of the delegate.

SC4: You must disclose appropriately any information of which the FCA or PRA would reasonably expect notice

- For the purpose of rule SC4, regulators in addition to the FCA and the PRA are those which have recognised jurisdiction in relation to activities to which COCON applies and have a power to call for information from the relevant person in connection with their function or the business for which they are responsible. This may include an exchange or an overseas regulator.

- SC4 applies to an SMF manager in addition to rule 3 in COCON 2.1.3R. Although, the rules have some overlap, they are different. Rule 3 normally relates to responses from individuals to requests from the regulator, whereas rule SC4 imposes a duty on SMF managers to disclose appropriately any information of which the appropriate regulator would reasonably expect, including making a disclosure in the absence of any request or enquiry from the appropriate regulator. An SMF manager is likely to have access to greater amounts of information of potential regulatory importance and to have the expertise to recognise when this may be something of which the appropriate regulator would reasonably expect notice.

- Where a person is responsible within the firm (individually or with other SMF managers) for reporting matters to the regulator, failing promptly to inform the regulator concerned of information of which they are aware and which it would be reasonable to assume would be of material significance to the regulator concerned, whether in response to questions or otherwise, constitutes a breach of rule SC4 in COCON 2.2.4R.

- If an SMF manager comes across a piece of information that is something in relation to which they think the FCA or PRA could reasonably expect notice, they should determine whether that information falls within the scope of their responsibilities (for an SMF manager, by virtue of that person's statement of responsibilities). If it does, then they should ensure that, if it is otherwise appropriate to do so, it is disclosed to the appropriate regulator. If it does not fall within the scope of their responsibilities then, in the absence of any reason to the contrary, they might reasonably assume that its disclosure to the appropriate regulator was being dealt with by the SMF manager with responsibility for dealing with information of that nature. If an SMF manager was not sure that the matter was being dealt with by another SMF manager, or if they were not sure whether this was in their area or not, the FCA would expect them to make enquiries to inform themselves, rather than disregard the matter.

- In determining whether or not a person's conduct complies with rule SC4 in COCON 2.2.4R, the factors which the FCA would expect to take into account include:
  (1) whether it would be reasonable for the individual to assume that the information would be of material significance to the regulator concerned;
  (2) whether the information related to the individual themselves or to their firm; and

(3) whether any decision not to report the matter was taken after reasonable enquiry and analysis of the situation.

Practical pointers on 'reasonable steps'

The steps that a Senior Manager should take ... are such steps as would have been taken by a competent Senior Manager at that time in that specific individual's position with that individual's role and responsibilities in all the existing circumstances. Senior Managers, when considering what steps to take, should also have regard to their existing statutory, common law and equitable obligations, including those set out in the Companies Act 2006, the Conduct Rules, the UK Corporate Governance Code, and the Model Code.[39]

Section 66B(5)(d) involves the PRA assessing (a) the steps that the specific Senior Manager actually took, against (b) such steps as the PRA considers that a Senior Manager, in that position, could reasonably have been expected to take to avoid the contravention occurring (or continuing). The PRA's expectations of the steps in (b) will necessarily depend on the circumstances as they existed at the time. It is not the PRA's intention to apply standards retrospectively or with the benefit of hindsight. However, examples of the considerations that the PRA may consider in forming its view of (b) can include:

- the size, scale and complexity of the firm;
- what the Senior Manager actually knew, or a Senior Manager in that position ought to have known (taking into account, among other factors, the length of time they have been in the role and handover arrangements to those new in a role);
- what expertise and competence the Senior Manager had, or ought to have possessed, at the time to perform his or her specific Senior Management Function;

---

[39] Paragraphs 5.1, 5.5 and 5.6 FCA: CP15/9, "Strengthening Accountability in Banking: A New Regulatory Framework for Individuals – Feedback on FCA CP14/13 / PRA CP14/14 and Consultation on Additional Guidance", March 2015.

- what steps the Senior Manager could have taken, considering what alternative actions might have been open to the Senior Manager at the time and the timeliness within which he or she could have acted;

- the actual responsibilities of that Senior Manager and the relationship between those responsibilities and the responsibilities of other Senior Managers in the firm (including in relation to any joint responsibilities or matrix-management structures);

- whether the Senior Manager delegated any functions, taking into account that any such delegation should be appropriately arranged, managed and monitored; and

- the overall circumstances and environment at the firm and more widely, in which such a Senior Manager was operating at the time. For example, where a Senior Manager was subject to competing priorities, the PRA may consider whether the way in which he or she prioritised them was informed by an appropriate risk assessment.

In relation to '(a)' and the steps that a Senior Manager actually took to avoid the contravention occurring or continuing, examples of the steps that may be considered to be reasonable actions, depending on the circumstances, could include:

- pre-emptive actions to prevent a breach occurring, including any initial reviews of the business or business area on taking up a Senior Manager function;

- implementing, policing and reviewing appropriate policies and procedures;

- awareness of relevant requirements and standards of the regulatory system;

- investigations or reviews of the Senior Manager's area of responsibilities;

- where a breach is continuing, any response taken to that breach;

- structuring and control of day-to-day operations, including ensuring any delegations are managed and reviewed appropriately. This includes in relation to any 'matrix-management' arrangements;

- obtaining appropriate internal management information, and critically *interrogating* and monitoring that information;
- raising issues, reviewing issues, and following them up with relevant staff, committees and boards;
- seeking and obtaining appropriate expert advice or assurance, whether internal or external;
- ensuring that the firm and/or relevant area has adequate resources, and that these are appropriately deployed, including for risk and control functions; and
- awareness of relevant external developments, including key risks.
- Evidence that the PRA might seek to obtain in respect of these kinds of matters could include:
  - board and board committee minutes,
  - minutes of other internal meetings;
  - Statements of Responsibilities and Responsibilities Maps;
  - organisation charts and information on reporting lines;
  - any other internal materials, for example, emails or telephone recordings; and
  - regulatory correspondence and interviews.

An SMF manager is guilty of misconduct further to section 66A(5) of the Act where:

(1) there has been (or continued to be) a contravention of a relevant requirement by the SMF manager's firm;

(2) at the time of the contravention, the SMF manager was responsible for the management of any of the firm's activities in relation to which the contravention occurred; and

(3) in a contested case, the FCA establishes points (1) and (2), above, in any proceedings before the RDC, a court or a tribunal, with the SMF manager as a party to the action; and

(4) the SMF manager does not satisfy the FCA that they had taken such steps as a person in their position could reasonably be expected to take to avoid the contravention by the firm occurring (or continuing) ...[40]

When determining, for the purposes of section 66A(5) of the Act, whether an SMF manager was responsible for the management of any of the firm's activities in relation to which a contravention of a relevant requirement by the firm occurred, the FCA will consider the full circumstances of each case.

A list of considerations that may be relevant for this purpose is set out below. This list is not exhaustive: there may be other considerations, not listed, that are relevant.

(1) The SMF manager's statement of responsibilities, including whether the SMF manager was performing an executive or non-executive role.

(2) The firm's management responsibilities map.

(3) How the firm operated, and how responsibilities were allocated in the firm in practice.

(4) The SMF manager's actual role and responsibilities in the firm, to be determined by reference to, among other things, the minutes of meetings, emails, interviews, telephone recordings and organisational charts.

(5) The relationship between the SMF manager's responsibilities and the responsibilities of other SMF managers in the firm.

Under section 66A(5)(d) of the Act, such steps as a person in the position of the SMF manager could reasonably be expected to take to avoid the firm's contravention of a relevant requirement occurring (or continuing) are:

such steps as a competent SMF manager would have taken:

(1) at that time;

---

[40] Draft handbook text DEPP 6.2.9-AG: CP15/9, "Strengthening Accountability in Banking: A New Regulatory Framework for Individuals – Feedback on FCA CP14/13 / PRA CP14/14 and Consultation on Additional Guidance", March 2015.

(2) in that specific individual's position;

(3) with that individual's role and responsibilities;

(4) in all the existing circumstances.

When determining whether or not an SMF manager satisfies the FCA under section 66A(5)(d) of the Act, that they had taken such steps as a person in their position could reasonably be expected to take to avoid the contravention of a relevant requirement by the firm occurring (or continuing), additional considerations to which the FCA would expect to have regard include, but are not limited to:

(1) the role and responsibilities of the SMF manager;

(2) whether the SMF manager exercised reasonable care when considering the information available to them;

(3) whether the SMF manager reached a reasonable conclusion on which to act;

(4) the nature, scale and complexity of the firm's business;

(5) the knowledge the SMF manager had, or should have had, of regulatory concerns, if any, relating to their role and responsibilities;

(6) whether the SMF manager, where they were aware of, or should have been aware of, actual or suspected issues where these involved possible breaches by their firm of relevant requirements relating to their role and responsibilities, took reasonable steps to ensure that they were dealt with in a timely and appropriate manner;

(7) whether the SMF manager acted in accordance with their statutory, common law and other legal obligations, including, but not limited to, the (Senior Manager) Conduct Rules (and other relevant rules) set out in the FCA Handbook, those set out in the Companies Act 2006, the Handbook (including COCON), and, if the firm was listed on the London Stock Exchange, the UK Corporate Governance Code and related guidance;

(8) whether the SMF manager took reasonable steps to ensure that any delegation of their responsibilities, where this was itself reasonable, was to an appropriate person, with the necessary

capacity, competence, knowledge, seniority or skill, and whether they took reasonable steps to oversee the discharge of the delegated responsibility effectively;

(9) whether the SMF manager took reasonable steps to ensure that the reporting lines, whether in the UK or overseas, in relation to the firm's activities for which they were responsible, were clear to staff and operated effectively;

(10) whether the SMF manager took reasonable steps to satisfy themselves, on reasonable grounds, that, for the activities for which they were responsible, the firm had appropriate policies and procedures for reviewing the competence, knowledge, skills and performance of each individual member of staff, to assess their suitability to fulfil their duties;

(11) whether the SMF manager took reasonable steps to assess, on taking up each of their responsibilities, and monitor, where this was reasonable, the governance, operational and risk management arrangements in place for the firm's activities for which they were responsible (including, where appropriate, corroborating, challenging, and considering the wider implications of the information available to them), and whether they took reasonable steps to deal with any actual or suspected issues identified as a result in a timely and appropriate manner;

(12) whether the SMF manager took reasonable steps to ensure an orderly transition when another SMF manager under their oversight or responsibility was replaced in the performance of that function by someone else;

(13) whether the SMF manager took reasonable steps to ensure an orderly transition when they were replaced in the performance of their function by someone else;

(14) whether the SMF manager took reasonable steps to understand and inform themselves about the firm's activities in relation to which they were responsible, including, but not limited to, whether they:

(a) permitted the expansion or restructuring of the business without reasonably assessing the potential risks;

(b) inadequately monitored highly profitable transactions, business practices, unusual transactions or individuals who contributed significantly to the profitability of a business area or who had significant influence over the operation of a business area;

(c) failed to obtain independent, expert opinion where appropriate from within or outside the firm;

(d) failed to seek an adequate explanation of issues within a business area, whether from people within that business area, or elsewhere within or outside the firm, if they were not an expert in that area; or

(e) failed to maintain an appropriate level of understanding about an issue or a responsibility that they delegated to an individual or individuals;

(15) whether the SMF manager took reasonable steps to ensure that where they were involved in a collective decision affecting the firm's activities for which they were responsible, where it was reasonable for the decision to be taken collectively, they informed themselves of the relevant matters before taking part in the decision, and exercised reasonable care, skill and diligence in contributing to the decision;

(16) whether the SMF manager took reasonable steps to follow the firm's procedures, where this was itself appropriate;

(17) how long the SMF manager had been in the role, with its responsibilities, and whether there was an orderly transition and handover when they took up the role and responsibilities; and

(18) whether the SMF manager took reasonable steps to implement (either personally or through a compliance department or other departments) adequate and appropriate systems and controls to comply with the relevant requirements and standards of the regulatory system for the activities of the firm.

KEY QUESTIONS TO CONSIDER

Reasonable steps

Questions

In any given situation, a Senior Manager might usefully ask 'what more could I reasonably have been expected to do in the circumstances?' Or, put another way, 'what could I reasonably be criticised for having not done?'

Comments

Following a regulatory breach by a firm, a Senior Manager considered responsible for the firm's activities/area in respect of which the contravention occurred will need to be in a position to demonstrate, if challenged by the Regulator under the Duty of Responsibility, that he or she has taken such reasonable steps as would have been taken by a competent Senior Manager at that time in that specific individual's position. Similarly, a Senior Manager being pursued under the (Senior Manager) Conduct Rules must also, in effect, be able to evidence 'reasonable steps'.

The need for a Senior Manager to be able to evidence 'reasonable steps' exists despite the fact that, technically, the burden of proof falls on the Regulator. In essence, this is a reflection of the fact that as soon as an allegation is made by the Regulator, the buck effectively passes to the Senior Manager. If the Senior manager cannot establish 'reasonable steps', the Regulator may seek to argue that its case is effectively made out. In such circumstances, the Senior Manager's only recourse may be to challenge the Regulator's contention before the Upper Tribunal (not an avenue that every Senior Manager will wish or be financially able to pursue).

Reasonable steps will include both pre-emptive and remedial actions.

When considering what constitutes 'reasonable steps', the Regulator will have regard to all applicable circumstances, including (without limitation): the Senior Manager's responsibilities; whether the Senior Manager exercised reasonable care and reached reasonable conclusions based on the information available; the nature, scale and complexity of the business; what knowledge and expertise the Senior Manager possessed (or should have possessed) at the time; and relevant regulatory requirements.

External assurance/input can often serve a useful purpose in this regard (see further below).

Importance of demonstrability

Recent experience suggests that senior individuals who are unable to corroborate their account with demonstrable evidence are unlikely to be able to satisfy the Regulator of the reasonableness of their conduct (and hence persuade the Regulator to drop any proposed enforcement action). In other words, the Regulator may well doubt whether an event really happened, if there is no supporting (ideally, contemporaneous) documentary evidence. An unfair working presumption perhaps, but reality nonetheless.

By way of example, the Regulator will expect to see challenge and consideration of clients' interests, risk and compliance feature sufficiently prominently in relevant board/committee minutes. In practice, the Regulator is unlikely to accept that clients' interests were appropriately discussed without contemporaneous documentary evidence to support such a contention.

Similarly, a delegating Senior Manager[41] would be well advised to ensure that there is an appropriate 'audit trail' serving as evidence of the effectiveness of their oversight of the delegate(s). Most obviously, this might be by way of routine email follow-ups to delegate meetings, briefly summarising the issues discussed, action points, time-frames, accountabilities, etc. Such a record would likely form a key element of a Senior Manager's rebuttal to any allegation that he or she failed to take reasonable steps to oversee the delegate(s) effectively (under SC3).

Where possible, relevant matters would be evidenced through meeting minutes,[42] file notes and other forms of contemporaneous

---

[41] Most Senior Managers will necessarily have to delegate.
[42] Many financial institutions have recently revisited the manner in which minutes are recorded – to ensure (amongst other things) that they are sufficiently balanced, comprehensive and reflective of all challenges.

documentary correspondence/records (such as emails following up meetings). While this does not, of course, mean that every last piece of dialogue, deliberation and thought process must be studiously recorded, it nevertheless requires an ongoing awareness of those matters or issues most likely (or with greatest potential) to attract subsequent regulatory scrutiny. As an informal rule of thumb, a Senior Manager might usefully consider whether the matter at hand has real potential to 'come back to bite' them. In many cases, this will be reasonably self-evident – one way or the other. Chapter 9 elaborates further on the topic of record-keeping.

Understanding/decision-making

Questions

- Could I comfortably summarise the firm's strategy, business model, product lines and customer base?
- Similarly, could I readily articulate the key risks faced by the firm and the attendant controls?
- In all honesty, do I consider that I possess the necessary skills and experience to carry out my agreed responsibilities?
- Have I gained a sufficient inherent understanding of the business in order for me to properly scrutinise the performance of management and deliver informed challenge?
- Am I comfortable that I receive an appropriate level of management information to enable me to properly discharge my responsibilities?
- Could I demonstrate to the Regulator, in respect of significant decisions taken, that all options available were discussed and duly considered? Would this be borne out in the relevant board or committee minutes?
- Am I confident that the relevant board/committee minutes would reflect the due consideration of clients' interests and conduct risk, as appropriate?
- Do I critically review management information provided and raise any 'red flags' or issues as appropriate? Could I explain to the Regulator how these are being (or have been) addressed and what follow-up reporting is provided?

- Am I alert to potentially troubling emerging trends/themes?
- Am I comfortable that any questions posed or challenges raised receive satisfactory responses?

Operating procedures

- Do I understand (and could I articulate at a high level) what operating procedures and systems have been implemented to ensure compliance with key regulatory requirements?
- Is a watching brief kept on such procedures and systems to ensure that they remain fit for purpose? In practice, what does this entail? For example, what form(s) of assurance are received, from whom and how regularly?
- Are there any legacy issues which remain unresolved? Is there any obvious scope for improvement?

Comments

Understanding: strategy and business model

The Regulator expects all Senior Managers to understand the business(es) for which they are responsible. Although they are not necessarily expected to be expert in all aspects of a firm's business, Senior Managers should nevertheless display a sound understanding of the firm's strategy, business model, customers and products.

A solid understanding of the firm's business is crucial to ensure that the fair treatment of customers and, more generally, conduct risk are considered both in the ordinary course of business and also in the context of strategic business decisions. For example, Senior Managers should not approve the expansion of new business or products without first ensuring that they fully understand the impact on the business and any additional risks posed to customers (and otherwise).

A Senior Manager's failure to understand (and be able to articulate at a high level) the key risks faced by the firm and the associated controls is likely to serve as a 'red flag' for the Regulator.

Management Information

When determining whether a Senior Manager has taken reasonable steps in respect of a regulatory breach by a firm, the Regulator will consider not only the knowledge that a Senior Manager had but also the knowledge they should have had at the relevant time. Senior Managers must therefore ensure that they are adequately informed about the business for which they are responsible.

It is essential that Senior Managers regularly receive and scrutinise all relevant management information provided. It follows that management information must be of the requisite quality to enable the Senior Manager to properly oversee his or her area of responsibility. The Regulator will expect a Senior Manager to address any deficiencies in the information received and seek further information and confirmations from relevant individuals where appropriate.

Importantly, management information must strike an appropriate balance: it should not be unwieldy and over-detailed; however, at the same time, it should be sufficiently instructive to enable a Senior Manager to obtain the necessary degree of visibility and oversight, and to make well-informed decisions.

For example, reports may consistently indicate that there are no issues to be addressed. In such circumstances, Senior Managers might question whether the management information provided is 'too good to be true'.

Where reviewing management information, Senior Managers should remain alert to any potentially problematic themes or trends that emerge which may be indicative of wider systemic issues, for example:

* Recurrent non-completion of mandatory training.
* Repeated breaches of internal policies and procedures (such as personal account dealing rules).
* Recurrent regulatory compliance issues (for instance, trade reporting errors; failure to adhere to internal policies, such as complaints handling; or CASS rule breaches).
* Frequent IT/systems issues.
* Recurrent instances of non-escalation of important issues.

- Repeated breach of Service Level Agreements by third parties.
- Repeated deadlines missed in the context of important projects.

Risk management

Questions

- Do I have a sufficiently strong grasp of the risk management framework – in particular, its design, operational effectiveness and any specific weaknesses? Could I articulate this framework in an interview with the Regulator?

- Do I properly understand (and could I readily summarise) both the compliance and operational risk assessment process(es)?

- More specifically, could I comfortably describe the firm's conduct risk management framework, risk appetite and tolerance, and how my firm defines 'conduct risk'?

- Are the risk management framework and controls periodically reviewed to ensure that they remain fit for purpose? Do I have the requisite visibility over the outputs of such reviews? Is there obvious room for improvement?

- Do I fully appreciate that I have a responsibility for implementing adequate and appropriate systems and controls to ensure regulatory compliance?

- Could I explain how the 3 Lines of Defence model operates within the firm and where I fit in?

- Am I satisfied (and can I demonstrate) that the risk profile for my area of responsibility is appropriate and reflects the firm's risk appetite?

- Do I understand (in broad terms) how my firm's Internal Capital Adequacy Assessment Process (ICAAP) is compiled?

- Could I explain what purpose(s) the ICAAP serves?

- Can I articulate the firm's risk appetite/tolerance, and how the firm ensures that it continues to operate within these parameters? Do I understand what 'checks and balances' exist to ensure that these parameters are respected?

Operational risk

- Do I really understand the operational risks inherent in the business and emanating from the firm's business model and strategy, and the associated systems of control? Are these risks and controls periodically assessed? How and by whom?
- Does the management information provided actually facilitate such an assessment?
- Do I have confidence in, and sufficient visibility over, the Operational Risk function?
- Do I fully understand how the business makes its money and the drivers of its primary source(s) of revenue?

Risk awareness

- Am I consciously alert to red flags – for example: unusual transactions or practices; worrying trends; inordinately profitable products; and unsatisfactory or implausible explanations from delegates or third party associates?
- Do I challenge and ask searching questions, where necessary – for example, around seemingly implausible explanations?

Employee cover

- Am I alive to the risks of allowing managerial posts to remain vacant without appropriate cover?

Comments

Risk management/Framework

The Regulator expects the firm's strategy to be supported by a statement of risk appetite which can be readily understood by the entire organisation. The board should both take ownership of such a statement and ensure that it is actively used when assessing risks and considering key business decisions.

As a matter of course, the Regulator will expect Senior Managers to have a sound understanding of the firm's risk management framework, risk appetite and tolerance, as well as its financial controls and remuneration model(s). These are topics that are frequently raised in regulatory interviews.

It will be important for an incoming Senior Manager to quickly get up to speed with the firm's overall risk and control environment, and form an initial assessment as to whether any obvious/significant issues exist. In respect of any legacy risk issues, Senior Managers should obtain assurance that these have been satisfactorily resolved.

A failure to display a sound understanding of the firm's risk management framework may serve as a red flag for the Regulator. The preparation of simple schematics illustrating the risk management framework may be a helpful tool for Senior Managers. Such schematics could serve a number of purposes, such as ensuring clarity, and identifying any gaps, anomalies or issues that need to be addressed. They might also serve as useful papers to be furnished to the Regulator (if appropriate) during a supervisory visit.

Senior Managers should therefore ensure that the firm's risk control framework is kept actively under review to ensure (amongst other things) consistency with the firm's risk appetite and as a check for ensuring that Senior Managers are receiving sufficient management information.

3 Lines of Defence model

Senior Managers should be able to articulate the firm's 3 Lines of Defence risk management model, and, at a high level, at least how it operates in practice.

Risk awareness

Senior Managers should continually be alert to any potential red flag issues, or emerging themes, trends or patterns which may be viewed as indicative of wider systemic concerns. By way of example, recurrences of the following types of issue/incident might well serve as red flags:

- repeated contraventions by a member of staff of internal policies or procedures;
- frequently missed deadlines on key projects;

- consistently substandard service from outsources;
- troubling staff survey results;
- high customer complaint rates;
- poor exit interview feedback;
- repeated trade reporting errors;
- especially high staff turnover in certain teams or departments;
- poor mandatory training attendance; and
- repeated/significant limit breaches.

Governance

Questions

- Do I have a sufficiently strong grasp of the governance framework – in particular, its design, operational effectiveness and any specific weaknesses? Could I articulate this framework in an interview with the Regulator?
- Am I clear as to my role(s) within the governance framework and how/where I fit into the grand scheme?
- Is the governance framework periodically reviewed to ensure that it remains fit for purpose? If so, by whom and how frequently? Do I have the requisite visibility over the outputs of such reviews?
- Could I explain how the 3 Lines of Defence model operates within the firm and where I reside?
- Are there too many committees, with overlapping responsibilities, within the governance framework?
- Are there any obvious gaps?
- Are committees appropriately constituted?
- Are all Terms of Reference clear, with no potential for confusion/ overlap?
- Could I readily explain (at a high level) the purpose and function of each key committee within the governance framework?
- Are issues being dealt with at the right level within the governance framework?

- Is there obvious room for improvement?

Oversight and escalation

- Am I comfortable that I would have sufficient visibility over any significant issues or incidents arising within my area of responsibility? Can I point to recent examples?
- In respect of my area of responsibility, can I articulate what formal escalation channels exist? Am I confident that these are widely known and observed?
- When was the last time that an issue was escalated to the board or relevant committee on which I sit?

Reporting lines

- Am I satisfied that reporting lines and accountabilities within my area of responsibility are sufficiently clear (and understood)?
- How easily could these be evidenced?

Role descriptions

- Are job descriptions in place for all relevant personnel within my area of responsibility?

Comments

Effective organisation and governance

Governance is (and will likely remain) a key area of focus for the Regulator. Accordingly, it will be important for Senior Managers to be able to describe (and display a sound understanding of) the firm's governance framework.

A key responsibility for all Senior Managers is to ensure that the business for which they are responsible is effectively organised. What constitutes effective organisation will depend on the firm's model, structure and operational set-up. The role of the Senior Manager will be to ensure that they are able to monitor and control the business for which they are responsible in a way which is proportionate to the firm's strategy and in accordance with its risk tolerance.

The preparation and maintenance of simple schematics illustrating both reporting lines and the allocation of responsibility could be a helpful tool for Senior Managers. Such schematics could serve a number of purposes, such as ensuring clarity and identifying any gaps, anomalies or issues that need to be addressed. They might also serve as useful papers to be provided to the Regulator (if appropriate) during a supervisory visit.

The (Senior Manager) Conduct Rules require a Senior Manager to ensure that the business of the firm for which he or she is responsible complies with the relevant regulatory requirements. A Senior Manager must therefore take reasonable steps to ensure that for each area of the business for which he or she is responsible there are appropriate policies and procedures for complying with regulatory requirements and that relevant staff are suitably trained.

On taking up his/her responsibilities, the Regulator expects a Senior Manager to assess, and monitor, the operational and risk management systems in place for his/her area of responsibility. Such an assessment is crucial in order for a Senior Manager to identify whether any obvious/ significant issues exist.

Delegation

Questions

- Am I satisfied that appropriate due diligence was undertaken prior to the delegation of a material issue, project or aspect of the business?

- When delegating, is sufficient demonstrable thought given to the delegate's capacity, expertise and experience to perform the delegated task(s)?

- How comfortable would I feel in articulating (and demonstrating) this to the Regulator?

- Am I satisfied that the firm has retained an appropriate understanding of any business or services delegated?

- What ongoing oversight is maintained over delegates and delegated issues/business? Is this effective or is there room for improvement? How is this evidenced?

Comments

Delegation of functions poses obvious risks to a Senior Manager's effective control of the business for which he or she is responsible.

In respect of delegation by the board, the Regulator will expect that any reserved matters are clearly specified, and that the manner in which executive management must report and escalate matters is well understood and appropriately documented.

In respect of any delegation by a Senior Manager, the Regulator will expect that the delegate was selected following appropriate consideration and that the Senior Manager maintains an appropriate degree of effective oversight of the delegated functions.

An ill-considered delegation, for example to an individual at an inappropriate level, may cause the Regulator to question a Senior Manager's exercise of responsibility.

Senior Managers should approach delegation with the understanding that although they may delegate the handling of a particular issue or aspect of the business, they cannot delegate their responsibility for it. They must therefore be comfortable that they receive sufficient periodic information in order to supervise the delegation effectively and to retain an adequate understanding of the services delegated.

A pre-delegation protocol, incorporating a practical checklist, might usefully be considered (if one does not already exist). Such a protocol might cover (amongst other things):

- the delegate's specifically relevant credentials and expertise, and proven track record;
- the delegate's capacity and capability for the role in question;
- (in respect of an external delegation) the form of agreement in place with the delegate – which would ordinarily be expected to include (amongst other things): provisions affording the delegating firm supervision/monitoring rights; periodic reporting/management

information requirements; appropriate termination rights; service level standards; and resource commitment; and

- (in respect of an internal delegation) an agreed reporting schedule providing for periodic reporting/management information; periodic catch-up meetings; and scheduled performance review sessions.

Regulatory awareness

Questions

- Do I fully appreciate the key regulatory requirements (and expectations) relevant to my area of responsibility? For example, am I familiar with any recently issued thematic reports, relevant to the firm's business?
- Could I comfortably articulate these to the Regulator, if required?
- Am I confident that any material regulatory developments are drawn to my attention in a timely manner? How do I ensure that any gaps resulting from regulatory changes are identified, and that appropriate action is taken to address such gaps?
- Are regulatory enforcement notices against other firms or individuals and other regulatory pronouncements (such as thematic reports) being actively monitored – to assess whether there is any potential application or 'read-across' onto (or lessons to be learned within) our business?
- Do I receive periodic (and meaningful) refresher training? When was my last training session?
- Do I have knowledge gaps, which need to be plugged?

Comments

Senior Managers are expected to have a strong grasp of (and be able to articulate) the regulatory environment in which they are operating. Periodic refresher training and awareness sessions (in particular, on regulatory hot topics) are now widely regarded as essential.

As relevant to their area of responsibility, Senior Managers should ensure that they: are kept abreast (in a timely manner) of pertinent regulatory developments; and have sufficient knowledge and expertise to help contextualise and identify any areas of concern.

Senior Managers should also ensure that the firm is actively monitoring regulatory developments and enforcement actions against other firms or individuals – to assess whether there is any potential application or read-across onto (or lessons to be learned within) the firm's own business or operations.

Staff regulatory awareness

Questions

- Do staff fully appreciate the key regulatory requirements (and expectations)?
- Could they articulate these to the Regulator, if required?
- Do staff receive periodic (and meaningful) refresher training? When was their last training session?
- Is there obvious room for improvement?

Comments

Senior Managers are responsible for ensuring the due compliance of their respective business area(s) with the requirements and standards of the regulatory system. A key aspect of this responsibility is ensuring the requisite level of staff awareness and understanding.

In practical terms, this is likely to involve periodic training and education sessions.

It is important that all such training is sufficiently relevant and tailored to the particular audience – to maximise attendee engagement and benefit. Conversely, poor quality/untailored training can often result in (self-defeating) disengagement.

Competence and expertise

Questions

- Do I, as a matter of course, assess the ongoing suitability of individuals working within my business area?

- Would I be comfortable in explaining to the Regulator the nature and extent of the measures that I take? Are these measures verifiable?
- Am I satisfied that appropriate policies and procedures are in place for reviewing the competence, skills, knowledge and performance of each relevant individual within my area of responsibility?
- Are these sufficiently clear and demonstrable?
- How comfortable would I feel in describing these to the Regulator?

Comments

In a similar vein, it is important for Senior Managers to keep a close watch on the ongoing suitability of individuals working within their business area(s) – particularly when the Senior Manager has been put on notice that an individual's competence or capability has been called into question.

Practically, this may be achieved through the implementation of appropriate policies and procedures, focused on the periodic review and assessment of staff competence and performance.

Use of experts

Questions

- Do I appreciate the value in obtaining an independent expert opinion, where appropriate – for example, where this may help to provide a further layer of (objective and professional) assurance, offer some important industry perspective or help to validate an approach taken?
- Do the potential benefits outweigh the costs?
- If ever challenged by the Regulator, would I regret not having suggested or sought such expert guidance?

Comments

Use of specialist advisors

Where appropriate, Senior Managers should consider whether it would be desirable to enlist the services of external specialists – for example, to: assist with the remediation of identified issues; help support/ validate a particular approach; provide a degree of independent assurance; and/or assist with the implementation of specific projects.

Senior Managers might prudently assume that they may be challenged on why independent advice or input was not sought in a specific scenario. Whilst the commissioning of external advisors is not a firm requirement as such, it is important for a Senior Manager to have a credible response and to be able to justify why external involvement was not considered necessary in the circumstances.

Pre-emptive measures and reactivity

Questions

- Where an issue arises, am I confident that the firm would respond decisively and robustly (and be seen to respond as such)?
- In respect of any breaches that have materialised, am I able to explain to the Regulator the remedial action taken?
- Would I be inclined to challenge and ask searching questions – for example, around provisional conclusions reached or assurances provided? Would I be able to evidence this, if challenged?

Comments

Robust reactivity

Following an identified issue in respect of a Senior Manager's area of responsibility, the Senior Manager must be able to demonstrate that timely, credible and effective action was taken. Depending on the circumstances, an investigation with possible input from independent advisors may be required in order to determine the root cause and assess any indication of systemic or endemic risk. Where an investigation is not undertaken or independent advice not sought, such a decision should be readily justifiable.

In considering responsive and remedial actions, a Senior Manager should be able to demonstrate that all viable options were duly considered, and to explain to the Regulator why the chosen response was considered the most appropriate course of action.

The Senior Manager responsible should ensure that any remedial actions are implemented effectively and in a timely manner. In particular, it will be important for the Senior Manager to receive informative updates/management information regarding the implementation and effectiveness of the remedial measures undertaken, so that progress can be actively monitored.

Importantly, any lessons to be learned should also be expressly considered.

Senior Managers should appreciate that their firm's response to an identified breach is likely to serve as a key cultural indicator for the Regulator.[43] It is therefore essential that any such response is seen to be sufficiently robust and can be readily evidenced.

Orderly transitions

Questions

- Am I sufficiently familiar with the orderly transition procedures, and do I understand my responsibilities in this regard?

Comments

Transitional periods present particular risks for firms and are obvious areas of potential challenge. Senior Managers are expected to ensure that their responsibilities and management are not compromised during transitional periods. Accordingly, Senior Managers should be comfortable that there are appropriate handover procedures in place, and that there are no gaps in responsibility or expertise. Such procedures might typically cover (amongst other things) requirements for: the preparation of comprehensive handover notes; and (where possible) a handover period, during which the existing and prospective role holder would work together to ensure a seamless transition.

---

[43] See further chapter 6.

Compliance function

Questions

For Senior Managers responsible for the Compliance function:

- Am I comfortable that the Compliance function has the necessary authority, resources, expertise and access to relevant management information?

- Does the Compliance Officer have clear reporting lines for updating and escalating compliance issues to the board?

- Does the board receive regular (and meaningful) compliance updates? Are these of an appropriate quality and detail?

- Am I comfortable with the adequacy of procedures to ensure that the persons involved in the Compliance function are not involved in the performance of services or activities they monitor?

- Am I satisfied that the methods for determining the remuneration of persons involved in the Compliance functions is Remuneration Code compliant and does not compromise objectivity?

- Am I comfortable that the compliance function is able to (and actually does) operate with the requisite independence?

Compliance monitoring

- Am I satisfied that the level of compliance monitoring activity (including nature, scope and frequency) is appropriate?

- How often is the sufficiency of compliance monitoring activity reviewed, and by whom? Am I satisfied that this is appropriate?

- Do I understand (and could I articulate) how the compliance monitoring programme is devised?

Compliance breaches

- Are material breaches escalated as appropriate to board/committee level and are they fully considered? Is explicit consideration given as to whether these breaches are (or may be) indicative of systemic issues? If so, is appropriate action taken?

- Do I challenge and ask searching questions, if necessary – for example, around seemingly implausible explanations or late reports?

- Is there a conscious focus on identifying the underlying root cause(s) of any significant compliance breaches? How does this focus materialise in practice? Is it documented?

- Are 'lessons learned' exercises undertaken where appropriate, as a matter of course?

Comments

Compliance

The Compliance function is regarded by the Regulator as a crucial independent safeguard for all firms. Accordingly, it will be important to be able to demonstrate, if challenged, that (amongst other things) the Compliance function: is adequately resourced; possesses the requisite expertise and experience; has sufficient stature, visibility and voice internally; operates truly independently, without fear of raising difficult issues; and reports appropriate information to the board and other relevant committees.

The Compliance function is responsible for both advising the business on its adherence with applicable rules and regulations and for monitoring the business's compliance therewith.

In practice, the quality of monitoring activity in particular can be somewhat variable. Unsurprisingly, therefore, the Regulator has taken a keen interest in the overall adequacy of a firm's compliance monitoring programme and related activity – and, indeed, may draw wider adverse inferences (for example, about a firm's risk management framework and general culture) from a perceived deficient approach.

It is vital that any compliance breaches identified are (and are seen to be) taken sufficiently seriously, and escalated to, and overseen at, an appropriately senior level within the governance hierarchy. For example, a significant issue involving substantive potential customer detriment would ordinarily be expected to be escalated up to the board. Conversely, where such an issue is not seen to have been raised to board level, questions may well be asked about the adequacy of a firm's governance arrangements and, more broadly, about the prevailing internal culture.

As a matter of course, demonstrable consideration should be given to a root cause analysis and an assessment as to whether the particular issue may be indicative of wider systemic concerns.

It is especially important, for example, that searching questions are seen to have been posed, explanations probed and lessons learned.

Disclosure to the Regulator

Questions

- Where relevant, am I sufficiently clear as to my responsibilities to disclose appropriately any information of which the Regulator would reasonably expect notice, and am I sufficiently clear as to the importance placed on this responsibility by the Regulator?
- Am I confident that I receive the requisite levels of information to enable me to discharge this responsibility?
- Do I fully appreciate that my responses to regulatory questions must be truthful and not misleading in any respect?

Comments

This responsibility falls upon those individuals within the firm who are responsible for reporting matters to the Regulator. Such person(s) must promptly inform the Regulator of information of which they are aware and which it would be reasonable to assume would be of material significance to the Regulator, whether in response to questions or otherwise.

The Regulator places great store on this particular responsibility as an important source of intelligence and information about firms. Accordingly,[44] a failure to discharge this responsibility may well be regarded as a serious contravention.

---

[44] And based on numerous published regulatory sanctions.

Culture

Questions

- Am I sufficiently clear as to the Regulator's cultural expectations?
- Am I clear as to my role and responsibility in this context?
- Do I appreciate that the Regulator can relatively easily attribute any serious issue(s) or misconduct to a poor culture – in respect of which I may be held ultimately responsible?
- Can I articulate the culture and cultural expectations within my firm?
- Am I satisfied that I foster the appropriate culture within my area(s) of responsibility? Can I evidence this? Can I show that this culture is consistent with the wider firm's values and expectations?
- Can I provide some illustrative examples of the measures taken to establish and maintain the desired culture?
- Can I provide examples of how the right 'tone from the top' is set and maintained?
- Similarly, can I describe how the right 'tone from the middle' is set and maintained?
- Can I articulate how my firm independently measures/assesses whether the firm (and its staff) are satisfying espoused cultural values and expectations in practice?
- Could I describe some of the key cultural indicators or metrics used in such an assessment?
- Am I confident that staff across the firm are on the same 'cultural wavelength' as the board? How do I gain this assurance?

New business opportunities

- Am I comfortable that there is sufficient focus on risk, culture and clients when the firm is contemplating new business opportunities? Is this readily evidenced?
- Is the management information provided sufficiently informative in this respect?

Comments

The Regulator expects the board to articulate and maintain a culture of risk awareness and ethical behaviour. Senior Managers must therefore play their part in ensuring that a strong client-centric and compliant culture pervades throughout the organisation. This will include (but not be limited to) ensuring that: (i) the requisite tone from the top is set and reiterated periodically; (ii) culture at all levels of the firm is regularly measured against an agreed set of cultural indicator metrics – to ensure that the day-to-day actions are matching the rhetoric; (iii) any cultural issues (or observed shortfalls against metrics) are appropriately addressed and that lessons are learned, where necessary; (iv) the root causes of any such issues are identified and remedied; and (v) any emerging themes or trends which may be indicative of cultural failings are identified and investigated.

The important topic of culture is considered further in chapter 6.

Illustrative hypothetical scenarios

The regulator has provided the following illustrative examples of scenarios in which it may consider taking enforcement action against a Senior Manager performing an executive SMF:

- A firm breaches its capital adequacy requirements as a result of a major loss in a key business unit that has repeatedly breached it's risk limits. The risk limits were discussed and set by the Risk Committee and the Board. In this situation, the Regulator might primarily consider whether there are grounds to sanction the appropriate Senior Manager(s), including Heads of the Key Business Areas and the Chief Risk Officer. If, however, the breaches are reported to the Board and/or the Risk Committee, the Regulator may also enquire whether the Board/Risk Committee discussed them and made ay recommendations.

- In an attempt to obtain Board approval for a new, riskier, lending strategy, a firm's senior executives submit incomplete and misleading management information to the Board which significantly downplays the risks of such a strategy. The CEO also suppresses any negative or questioning advice on this issue, and consequently the Board approves the strategy which, six months later, causes the firm to breach a number of rules in the Risk Control section of the Regulator's rulebook.

- A firm's management fails to monitor the provision of services by a third party under an outsourcing agreement resulting in an operational risk crystallising in breach of a rule in the Regulators rulebook.

B. SPECIFIC ROLES

This section focuses on the functions of Chief Executive Officer; Director; Non-executive Director; and Compliance Oversight, and offers some role-specific guidance, having regard (among other things) to any lessons to be learned from relevant published enforcement actions.

The cases summarised in this section are not intended to be comprehensive accounts – rather, they are designed to provide the reader with a good sense of the type of conduct that has attracted regulatory criticism and sanction. It can be assumed that similar or analogous future conduct would likely result in adverse regulatory scrutiny.

CEOs

The importance of an incoming CEO undertaking an initial assessment (of the design and operational effectiveness of the governance and risk management frameworks) was underscored in the seminal *Pottage* case summarised below. Indeed, as can be seen, the initial assessment conducted by Mr Pottage formed the key basis upon which he was found to have taken the necessary 'reasonable steps'.

John Pottage v The Financial Services Authority, Upper Tribunal, 2012 – 'reasonable steps' taken

John Pottage held the CF3 (CEO) and CF8 (apportionment and oversight) functions at UBS Wealth Management (UK) Ltd, which was authorised by the Financial Services Authority (FSA). The FSA held that Mr Pottage had breached APER Principle 7, in that he had failed to take reasonable steps to ensure that the business of the firm complied with the relevant requirements and standards of the regulatory system. In particular, the FSA considered that the measures taken by Mr Pottage (in response to identified warnings and failings) from the date of his appointment as CEO (in September 2006) through to July 2007 were insufficient and, therefore, unreasonable. In essence, the FSA's case was based on the premise that Mr Pottage should have appreciated sooner than he did that there were serious flaws in UBS's systems and controls (as subsequently acknowledged by the Tribunal), and should have acted sooner to review and remediate the situation. Additionally, the FSA argued that Mr Pottage had not gone far enough and had been too accepting of assurances received.

Famously, Mr Pottage appealed and succeeded in overturning the FSA's findings before the Upper Tribunal. In essence, the Tribunal found that Mr Pottage had indeed taken reasonable steps and could not therefore be said to have breached APER Principle 7. In particular, he had undertaken an initial assessment (upon becoming CEO), during which he:

- conducted detailed interviews with management committee members;
- held meetings with senior staff concerned with risk management and Legal, Risk and Compliance;
- discussed teams and roles with the Head of Risk and Compliance;
- met the global heads of Legal, Risk and Compliance;
- met with Group Internal Audit and discussed its plans;
- met the COO to discuss operational issues;
- consulted his predecessor, who had not put him on notice of any matters of particular concern requiring his attention; and
- met the business unit head to understand key issues.

Further, Mr Pottage had also proactively addressed problems as they emerged. For instance, he had:

- appointed a new Head of Risk;
- reviewed and enhanced client money controls;
- commissioned a peer review of operations and replaced senior staff;
- added Risk to Executive Committee agendas;
- engaged a 'Big Four' accountancy firm to carry out an independent review of asset reconciliations;
- instigated a review of adviser training; and
- introduced solutions to address serious transgressions.

In overruling the FSA's initial determination against Mr Pottage, the Tribunal concluded that:

(i) Mr Pottage's initial assessment was reasonable – and that there was insufficient information apparent to him to indicate that he needed to undertake a more comprehensive investigation earlier on (as the FSA had suggested he ought to have done); and

(ii) Mr Pottage had investigated every identified control failure, instituted remedies and took steps to bolster the firm's controls.

In short, Mr Pottage had taken the requisite reasonable steps, and could not reasonably have been expected to go further.

The outcome of *Pottage* can be contrasted with the FSA's case against John Cummings.

John Cummings – where the steps taken were not 'reasonable'

Mr Cummings was the Chief Executive of the Corporate Division of HBOS and held a CF1 (director) function.

After its acquisition of HBOS, Lloyds Banking Group subsequently required a state-backed multi-billion-pound bailout in order to remain solvent. The bailout was widely attributed (in part at least) to the financial situation of HBOS's Corporate Division, regarded as the highest risk business area within HBOS.

The FSA alleged that Mr Cummings had instigated numerous transactions with weak lending criteria or aggressive credit structures, at a time when there were serious shortcomings in the Corporate Division's control framework. As the individual with specific responsibility for the Division's strategy and performance, its overall control framework and for managing risks, Mr Cummings ought to have appreciated these failings, and had thereby failed to manage the Division's credit risk appropriately. Moreover, any corrective measures taken by Mr Cummings simply did not go far enough. While the FSA acknowledged that Mr Cummings had not designed the controls and necessarily relied on others, he had nevertheless failed to: exercise proper oversight; heed internal warnings from Group Risk; and ensure that systems and controls were fit for purpose. In the FSA's view, he had also:

• provisioned over-optimistically, despite knowing that impaired transactions were not being appropriately assessed; and

- presided over an environment/culture in which risk management was regarded as an unhelpful business constraint; risk was effectively subordinated to revenue; management oversight was poor; and management information weak.

In short, the FSA concluded that Mr Cummings had not acted reasonably, in that he failed to take adequate measures to bolster the Corporate Division's risk management framework and continued with a high-risk strategy regardless. In other words, Mr Cummings ought reasonably to have done more than he did – in particular, he should have:

- ensured that stressed transactions were properly evaluated;
- monitored asset performance and ensured that it was appropriately accounted for;
- mitigated the key risks of weak underwriting and inadequate distribution;
- set prudent targets; and
- improved credit quality.

Cummings can be differentiated from *Pottage* on two principal grounds:

(i) while Mr Pottage expressly acknowledged deficiencies and proactively sought to address them, it appears that Mr Cummings adopted a more passive (and comparatively disinterested) approach; and

(ii) Mr Cummings saw no need to adjust his Division's business model, despite the various red flags concerning its inherent (and unsatisfactorily mitigated) risks. In contrast, Mr Pottage implemented various business model enhancements in order to address the perceived weaknesses.

In summary, while Mr Pottage remained on the front foot throughout, this could not be said of Mr Cummings, who played an altogether more passive role in events. Ultimately, this appears to have been a key factor behind the differing outcomes.

Of course, the precise nature and extent of any such initial assessment will vary, dependent upon the type, scale and relative complexity of the business. Additionally, a key determinant of the scope and depth of any initial review will be the significance and magnitude of any known compliance or risk issues. Accordingly, a CEO will be expected to have undertaken a proportionately wider and more rigorous review where known material issues exist.

Similarly, when there is an indication – albeit not yet confirmed – of risk or compliance issues, the CEO will be regarded as being on notice, and will therefore be expected to take prompt steps to understand the true position. Again, the nature and extent of these investigatory measures will depend proportionately on the type of issue concerned.

Barry Tootell (2016) – failure to take 'reasonable steps'

A very recent case involving a CEO provides a further sense of conduct deemed 'unreasonable' by the Regulator.

In August 2015, the Co-operative Bank was publicly censured for, amongst other things, failing to have in place adequate risk management systems.

Mr Tootell, CFO and later CEO of the Co-operative Bank, was found to have failed to act with due skill, care and diligence. In particular, Mr Tootell was centrally involved in a culture within the bank which encouraged prioritising the short-term financial position of the firm at the cost of taking prudent and sustainable actions to secure the bank's longer-term capital position.

Further, Mr Tootell did not take adequate steps to ensure that the banking risk team for which he was ultimately responsible was properly structured and organised to enable it to provide proper independent challenge and guidance to the first-line business of the bank. Accordingly, he was also 'knowingly concerned' in the Co-operative Bank's breach of its obligation to take reasonable steps to organise its affairs responsibly and effectively, with adequate risk management systems.

Mr Tootell also failed to:

*   properly oversee a major due diligence process to ensure that it adequately identified and documented risks;

- escalate risks in accordance with risk management protocols;
- exercise adequate oversight to ensure development of a clear strategy for a business area which had been identified as a significant risk; and
- ensure that a remedial project progressed with the requisite urgency and pace; and to ensure that effective targets and milestones were set.

Keith Alderson (2016) – failure to take 'reasonable steps'

Mr Alderson worked alongside Mr Tootell, as Director of Corporate Banking and later the Managing Director of the Corporate and Business Banking Division.

Mr Alderson was found not to have taken reasonable steps to ensure that the Co-operative Bank adequately assessed the risks rising across the Britannia Corporate Loan Book (following the bank's merger with Britannia). Amongst other things, Mr Alderson:

- failed to ensure that the bank adequately assessed the inherent risks of the acquired loan book;
- failed to escalate these risks to ExCo and formal risk management forums;
- failed to act in a timely manner to explore options for an alternative strategy (when the existing strategy was known to be flawed);
- failed to take reasonable steps to ensure that the first line of defence took an adequate approach to the management of risk;
- failed to take reasonable steps to ensure that the available management information was sufficient to monitor compliance with systems and controls; and
- presided over a culture which created an environment in which some staff felt under pressure to meet stipulated impairment forecasts, which resulted in over-optimistic decisions being made on impairment budgets, forecasts and provisions.

Other 'take-aways' from recent enforcement cases involving CEOs

While every case will turn on its own unique set of facts and circumstances, it is nevertheless possible to discern certain themes from recent enforcement cases brought against CEOs:

- the need for swift and credible responses to known issues or warning signs – CEOs must avoid any perception that issues are not being treated sufficiently seriously and with the requisite urgency, as illustrated by the *Pottage* and *Cummings* cases; and

- any perception that clients' interests and/or risks are being effectively subordinated to profitability considerations may prove to be decidedly unhelpful; CEOs must not be seen to be pursuing profits at all costs.

Culture

The topical subject of culture is covered in chapter 6. It is noteworthy that, under the SMR, the specific Prescribed Responsibility for *"overseeing the adoption of the firm's culture in the day-to-day management of the firm"* is expected to be allocated to the CEO. The CEO is therefore arguably at greatest risk from perceived cultural failings. Chapter 6 is therefore of particular relevance.

Attestations

Regulatory attestations are considered in chapter 7. For present purposes, it is simply worth noting that the majority of attestation requests to date have – perhaps unsurprisingly – been addressed to CEOs. Accordingly, CEOs would be well advised to consider carefully the import of chapter 7 – especially since attestations represent arguably the single greatest avenue of potential regulatory exposure for Senior Managers.

Directors

The heightened regulatory focus on senior individual accountability has prompted many regulated firm boards to reassess the duality of their respective legal and regulatory responsibilities. Chapter 8 highlights the apparent divergence between the legislative requirements applicable to directors of regulated entities and prevailing regulatory expectations. In essence, this divergence arises out of the fact that – broadly speaking – relevant legal requirements are underpinned by shareholders' interests, whereas regulatory expectations serve to the principal benefit of clients.[45]

NEDs

While it might be said that NEDs are perhaps less obvious or likely targets for the Regulator (than, say, CEOs), they are by no means immune from regulatory interest. For example, in 2013, Angela Burns (a NED) was fined and banned for failing to act with integrity. Among other things, Ms Burns was criticised for failing to disclose conflicts of interest and providing misleading information.

Further, with such a strong regulatory focus on culture and challenge, NEDs would be well advised to ensure that they are actually fulfilling the role expected of them by the Regulator – for example:

- gaining a sufficient understanding of the business to allow them to scrutinise effectively the performance of management and to deliver informed challenge;

- being satisfied that the management information being provided to the board is adequate and appropriate to support decision-making;

- challenging that management information – particularly if, for example, it is consistently indicating that everything is fine;

- ensuring that the board and/or committees which they chair:

  - meet with sufficient frequency;

  - foster an open, inclusive discussion which challenges executives where appropriate; and

  - devote sufficient time and attention to matters within their remit which are relevant to the firm's safety and soundness;

- reporting to the main board on the committee's activities;

---

[45] And, to a degree, the wider market.

- providing robust and insightful challenge to executive management on all aspects of the business, including culture. For example, on strategic business decisions, NEDs would be expected to be challenging senior management to ensure that the potential impact on clients and their fair treatment are considered from the outset; and

- ensuring that, where necessary, their challenge results in meaningful responsive actions and identification of root causes.

Any perceived failure to do so might just tempt the Regulator to launch a convenient enforcement action, used to send a warning message to the wider NED population in furtherance of its continued 'senior individual accountability' strategy.

Chairmen

More specifically, the Regulator expects chairmen to:

- seek to remain appraised of matters relating to the board and its individual committees by, for instance, having regular discussions with the Chairs of the Audit, Remuneration and Risk Committees outside board meetings; and

- commit a significantly larger proportion of their time to their functions than other NEDs. In particular, NEDs of major firms are expected not to have or take on additional commitments which may interfere with the fulfilment of those responsibilities to the firm under the SMR.

Chapter 5 considers in further detail the regulatory expectations and responsibilities of NEDs and, crucially, how personal regulatory risk might be managed in practice.

Compliance oversight

A number of enforcement cases have been brought against CF10s over recent years, several of which have involved questionable integrity and competence[46] – for example, knowingly providing incorrect or misleading information to the Regulator.[47]

---

[46] For example, *Ten-Holter* (2012), *Hughes* (2014), *Kraft* (2015) and *Wills* (2015).
[47] *Wills* (2014).

Additionally, the following (non-exhaustive) scenarios have obvious potential to attract adverse regulatory attention:

- failure to inform the Regulator of notifiable events;
- failure to challenge the business or a business decision, when given sufficient reason to believe that there is a material risk of non-compliance[48];
- failure to identify evident issues during monitoring activity;
- failure to action (or to cause to be actioned) any such issues, as appropriate;
- failure to act upon reasonable suspicions;
- inappropriate delegation (and subsequent monitoring thereof)[49];
- failure to seek appropriate advice/support;
- failure to raise any material compliance-related concerns with relevant stakeholders;
- failure to adequately assess the compliance risks of the business[50];
- failure to act appropriately upon any concerns raised by others;
- failure to ensure that the business is kept appropriately abreast of relevant regulatory developments[51];
- failure to formulate appropriately focused compliance monitoring plans[52];
- failure to identify serious weaknesses in operational controls and a lack of appropriate knowledge among staff;
- failure to inform senior management of any concerns, or resolve issues, about the effectiveness/resourcing of the Compliance function[53]; and
- failure to report material issues to the relevant individual(s)/committee(s) within the governance and risk frameworks.

---

[48] For example, see *Kraft* (2015) and *Ten-Holter* (2012).
[49] For example, *Unwin* (2012) and *Hughes* (2014).
[50] For example, *Kraft* (2015).
[51] For example, *Edwards* (2011).
[52] For example, *Hales* (2016).
[53] For example, *Kraft* (2015).

Those responsible for Compliance oversight should appreciate that the Regulator will not shy away from holding them to account by bringing individual enforcement actions where appropriate. The above scenarios provide an instructive (albeit non-exhaustive) guide to particular areas of personal exposure.

5

NON-EXECUTIVE DIRECTORS

INTRODUCTION

This chapter relates exclusively to NEDs and considers, in turn, the relevant backdrop, the regulatory expectations, the scope of responsibility and managing personal regulatory exposure under the SMR.

Backdrop: NEDs under the SMR

The Regulator has expressly acknowledged[54] the

"fundamentally different roles of executives and non-executives ... and that within the non-executive there are a range of roles and therefore responsibilities."

"The primary role of all NEDs is independent oversight and challenge of the Executive ... the Chairman, SIDs and Committee Chairmen have a specifically defined mandate ... therefore the [Regulator] considers it important that the SMR regime as a whole captures these key NEDs within its scope."

On this basis, the Regulator has drawn a distinction between (i) NEDs who occupy any of the following roles (Non-notified or in-scope NEDs): Chairman, Senior Independent Director and Committee Chairs; and (ii) all other NEDs (Notified NEDs). Notified NEDS will not be Senior Managers, but will nevertheless be required to comply with Conduct Rules 1–5 (inclusive) and Senior Manager Conduct Rule 4.

It follows, therefore, that the Regulator will have the ability to pursue Notified NEDs for breach of applicable (Senior Manager) Conduct Rules.

As a general matter, the regulator expects the Statements of Responsibilities of Non-notified (that is, in-scope) NEDs to be less

---

[54] See, for instance, paragraph 2.11 of CP7/15.

extensive than those of executive Senior Managers. However, firms can and, where appropriate, should add responsibilities not captured in the Regulator's rules to the Statement of Responsibilities of relevant non-executive Senior Managers. For instance, a firm may wish to make the Chairman responsible for succession planning.

Some Conduct Rules apply to NEDs in respect of their limited duties only. By way of example, the chair of the Remuneration Committee is likely to discharge his or her responsibilities under SM2 if he or she takes reasonable steps to ensure that the Remuneration Committee complies with the requirements of SYSC 19A, and remains free from undue executive interference in its decision-making.[55]

However, other Conduct Rules – such as the duty to act with integrity – apply to NEDs and executive Senior Managers in very similar ways.

The Regulator regards the requirement to be *"'open and cooperative'"* with a firm's regulators and *"to disclose appropriately any information of which the regulator would reasonably expect notice"* to be of particular importance for NEDs:

"If any director has concerns about the firm or its management and governance, the regulator will expect them to press for action to remedy the matter and, if those concerns are not addressed, to alert the [Regulator] ... This is why the regulator required firms to ensure that all NEDs, including those outside of scope of the SMR, observe SM4."

---

[55] Pursuant to SYSC 7.1.22R.

1. Regulatory expectations of NEDs

The table below consolidates PRA (*see* blue *text*), FCA (*see* red *text*) and joint PRA and FCA (*see* green *text*) expectations of NEDs under the Senior Managers Regime.

The table is followed by some key questions for NEDs to consider in addressing these regulatory expectations; alongside some insight and commentary.

PRA AND FCA PRONOUNCEMENTS

General

The SMR's emphasis on individual responsibilities is not, however, intended to undermine the collegiate, legal and regulatory responsibilities of the Board, which will retain ultimate decision making power and authority over all aspects of the firm's affairs.

The role of a Board sub-committee is to support the Board. The committees are accountable to the Board, but should not relieve the Board of any of its responsibilities.[57]

The potential accountability of NEDs in scope of the SMR is restricted to those activities for which they are responsible.[58]

Role of NED as Board/committee chair

Ensuring that the Board and/or the committees which they chair:

* meet with sufficient frequency;

* foster an open, inclusive discussion which challenges executives where appropriate; and

---

[56] Joint PRA and FCA, paragraph 2.6 of FCA CP14/13 / PRA CP14/14, "Strengthening Accountability in Banking: A New Regulatory Framework for Individuals", July 2014.
[57] PRA, paragraph 3.1 of the Appendix to CP18/5, "Corporate Governance: Board Responsibilities", May 2015.
[58] PRA, paragraph 2.31 of Supervisory Statement SS28/15, "Strengthening Individual Accountability in Banking", September 2016.

- devote sufficient time and attention to matters within their remit which are relevant to the firm's safety and soundness.

Helping to ensure that the Board or committee and its members have the information necessary to perform their tasks.

Facilitating the running of the Board or committee to assist it in providing independent oversight of executive decisions.

Reporting to the main Board on the committee's activities.

Although the SMR requires NEDs to take on individual responsibilities, the PRA views the regime and its application as consistent with the principle of collective decision-making.[59]

Chairmen

More specifically, the Regulator expects Chairmen to:

- seek proactively to remain appraised of matters relating to the Board and its individual committees by, for instance, having regular discussions with the Chairs of the Audit, Remuneration and Risk Committees outside Board meetings; and

- commit a significantly larger proportion of their time to their functions than other NEDs. In particular, NEDs of major firms are expected not to have or take on additional commitments which may interfere with the fulfilment of those responsibilities to the firm under the SMR.

Culture

The Board should articulate and maintain a culture of risk awareness and ethical behaviour for the entire organisation to follow in pursuit of its business goals. The [Regulator] expects the culture to be embedded with the use of appropriate incentives, including, but not limited to, remuneration, to encourage and enforce the behaviours the Board wishes to see, and for this to be actively overseen by the Board. The non-executives have a key role to play in holding

---

[59] PRA, paragraphs 2.31 and 2.36 of Supervisory Statement SS28/15, "Strengthening Individual Accountability in Banking", September 2016.

management to account for embedding and maintaining this culture.[60]

The role of a NED performing the general NED role is to:

(1) provide effective oversight and challenge; and

(2) help develop proposals on strategy.

To deliver this, their responsibilities include:

(1) attending and contributing to board and committee meetings and discussions;

(2) taking part in collective board and committee decisions, including voting and providing input and challenge; and

(3) ensuring they are sufficiently and appropriately informed of the relevant matters prior to taking part in board or committee discussions and decisions.

Other key roles of a NED include:

(1) scrutinising the performance of management in meeting agreed goals and objectives;

(2) monitoring the reporting of performance;

(3) satisfying themselves on the integrity of financial information;

(4) satisfying themselves that financial controls and systems of risk management are robust and defensible;

(5) scrutinising the design and implementation of the remuneration policy;

(6) providing objective views on resources, appointments and standards of conduct; and

(7) being involved in succession planning.[61]

---

[60] PRA, paragraph 3.1 of the Appendix to CP18/15, "Corporate Governance: Board Responsibilities", May 2015.
[61] FCA, Handbook text COCON 1 Annex 1G.

KEY QUESTIONS TO CONSIDER

Scope of responsibility

Questions

- Am I comfortable that I have sufficient oversight of the activities for which I am responsible?
- Are my responsibilities documented clearly and accurately? (See chapter 2)
- In reality, am I also entrusted with certain responsibilities which are not documented?
- Have I assumed de facto responsibility for certain matters, without these being formally reflected/documented?

Comments

The Regulator will consider a NED to be responsible for both the Prescribed Responsibilities allocated to him or her as well as any additional responsibilities introduced at the initiative of the firm. The Regulator will assess a NED's scope of responsibility by reference to all applicable circumstances. Whilst the Statement of Responsibilities and Responsibilities Map are clearly key considerations, **these will not be determinative where the practical reality is different**. In other words, the Regulator will look beyond the documentation to the actualities.

Board/committee meetings

Questions

- Does the board/committee meet with sufficient frequency and duration to allow for effective oversight and challenge?
- Is there **real** opportunity for inclusive discussion and challenge to executives? For example, is the board or committee effectively dominated by one individual? Would I feel comfortable if the Regulator was a 'fly on the wall' at relevant meetings? If not, what would I feel most anxious about? What would I like to improve?

Comments

The Regulator now commonly requires sight of board/committee papers and minutes, and periodically requests to attend and observe such meetings in person. Amongst other things, the Regulator will be assessing whether there is sufficient demonstrable understanding and challenge by the NEDs.

The Regulator will also likely focus on evidence that the Executive are effectively being held to account, and that customers' interests really are being put at the forefront of consideration and afforded due weight. Conversely, the Regulator is likely to take a dim view of any perception that clients' interests are being effectively subordinated to the commercial interests of the firm and/or its shareholder(s).

Management information

Questions

- Is the management information provided to me sufficiently informative? Is it unwieldy and unfathomable? Is it provided in good time to enable me to properly digest it?
- Am I confident that I have access to all relevant management information and external information – to ensure that I am fully appraised? In all honesty, am I provided with the information required to enable me to hold the Executive to account? Do I have any sense that certain potentially relevant information is being withheld?

Comments

Without sufficiently detailed management information, NEDs will not be properly equipped to perform their role. However, overly granular and unwieldy management information can prove to be counter-productive, and has been seen to attract regulatory criticism. Therefore, a sensible balance must be struck in practice. The board/committee secretariat should be constructively responsive to any suggestions in this regard.

Chairmen

Questions

- [Chairmen only] Do I catch up frequently enough outside of board meetings with the chairs of the various board committees? Am I comfortable that I receive as much intelligence from these committees as I should to ensure that I am properly appraised?

- [Chairmen only] Do I have sufficient available time to fulfil my Chairman role and 'do it justice'?

Comments

Arguably, of all NEDs, Chairmen are likely to attract most Regulatory interest. Accordingly, it will be important for Chairmen to ensure that they are sufficiently well 'plugged-in' to the various committees, through informal dialogue with their respective chairs.

Culture

Questions

- Do I fully appreciate the Regulator's cultural expectations and 'where the Regulator is coming from' in this regard?

- Am I comfortable that the firm is doing enough to ensure that an appropriate risk and compliance culture is embedded throughout (that is, at all operational levels of) the firm?

- How does the firm periodically check that it is practising what it preaches on culture? Is this adequate?

- Should my firm be undergoing a cultural change programme?

- Are the right cultural indicators being used as metrics?

- Are we spotting trends or themes which may be regarded as indicative of a poor culture?

- How easily would/could we rebut any suggestion that our culture was flawed or otherwise inadequate? What exactly would we point to in support of this?

Comments

As discussed further in chapter 6, culture is (and will likely remain) a key area of the Regulator's focus, with 'cultural attribution' now a real threat. Amongst other things, chapter 6 contains some practical pointers for Senior Managers in the context of culture. NEDs are expected to play an important role in overseeing that an appropriate culture is embedded and maintained.

Time/resourcing

Questions

- Am I able to dedicate sufficient time and attention to my NED role? For instance, am I continually struggling to digest board/ committee packs ahead of meetings?

- In truth, do I have too many competing priorities (for example, other NED roles) which are proving difficult to juggle?

Understanding of risk and control frameworks, etc

As a matter of course, the Regulator will expect NEDs to have a sound understanding of the firm's financial controls and remuneration model(s), together with risk management and conduct risk frameworks. Indeed, these are topics frequently raised at regulatory interviews with NEDs.

Awareness of relevant regulatory developments

NEDs should also keep (or be kept) abreast of relevant regulatory developments, and should have a good general appreciation of the regulatory environment in which their firm is operating.

2. Determining a NED's scope of responsibility

The table below consolidates the relevant PRA (*see* blue *text*) and FCA (*see* red *text*) provisions in relation to the determination of a NED's scope of responsibility. The table is followed by some key questions for NEDs to address; alongside some insights and commentary.

PRA AND FCA PRONOUNCEMENTS

Whether a Senior Manager is or is not responsible for managing any of the firm's relevant activities will be a question of fact. Statements of Responsibility and Responsibilities Maps should be relevant evidence but the PRA may look beyond these if it considers it appropriate.[62]

When determining, for the purposes of section 66A(5) of the Act, whether an SMF manager was responsible for the management of any of the firm's activities in relation to which a contravention of a relevant requirement by the firm occurred, the FCA will consider the full circumstances of each case. A list of considerations that may be relevant for this purpose is set out below. This list is not exhaustive: there may be other considerations, not listed, that are relevant.

(1) The SMF manager's statement of responsibilities, including whether the SMF manager was performing an executive or non-executive role.

(2) The firm's management responsibilities map.

(3) How the firm operated, and how responsibilities were allocated in the firm in practice.

(4) The SMF manager's actual role and responsibilities in the firm, to be determined by reference to, among other things, the minutes of meetings, emails, interviews, telephone recordings and organisational charts.

(5) The relationship between the SMF manager's responsibilities and the responsibilities of other SMF managers in the firm.[63]

---

[62] PRA, paragraph 2.71 of Supervisory Statement SS28/15, "Strengthening Individual Accountability in Banking", July 2015.
[63] Draft handbook text DEPP 6.2.9 CG: CP 15/9, "Strengthening Accountability in Banking: A New Regulatory Framework for Individuals – Feedback on FCA CP14/13/PRA CP14/14 and Consultation on Additional Guidance", March 2015.

KEY QUESTIONS TO CONSIDER

Statement of Responsibilities

Questions

- Is my Statement of Responsibilities sufficiently clear and accurately reflective of what I signed up for? Are there any ambiguities that might usefully be clarified?
- Is the firm's Responsibilities Map consistent and reconcilable with my Statement of Responsibilities?
- Is my Statement of Responsibilities consistent with the terms of reference of the committees on which I sit?
- Are my Statement of Responsibilities and the Responsibilities Map consistent with the actual responsibilities I undertake in practice? In reality, am I also entrusted with, or have I assumed, certain responsibilities which are not documented?
- Do board/committee minutes appropriately reflect my responsibilities? Or might they, for example, present an impression that I am responsible for more than I have signed up to?

Comments

A NED should review his or her Statement of Responsibilities carefully to ensure that it is clear, unambiguous and reflective of the NED's agreed remit.

NEDs should also check that their Statements of Responsibilities are entirely consistent with: (i) the terms of reference of the committees to which they belong; and (ii) the Responsibilities Map.

Substance over form

The regulator will assess a NED's scope of responsibility by reference to all applicable circumstances. Whilst the Statement of Responsibilities and Responsibilities Map are clearly key considerations, **they will not be determinative where the practical reality is different**. In other words, the Regulator will look beyond the documentation to the actualities.

NEDs might therefore usefully review, periodically, whether their Statements of Responsibilities continue to represent reality. Any perceived discrepancies should be raised and resolved, as lack of clarity is not in the interests of either the NED or the firm (and runs contrary to one of the underpinning principles of the SMR).

Assuming de facto responsibility

NEDs should also remain vigilant to ensure that they do not inadvertently assume any additional responsibilities to which they did not originally agree or sign up. For example, this may arise if a NED is asked to take on a particular oversight role, or where a NED voluntarily assumes additional responsibilities which go beyond his or her formally agreed remit.

3. Managing personal regulatory exposure

There are a number of ways in which the Regulator can pursue an in-scope NED under the regulatory system[64] (once the SRM has come into force) – namely, where the NED concerned: (i) can be shown (by the Regulator) to have been 'knowingly concerned' in a contravention of a relevant regulatory requirement by the firm; (ii) can be shown (by the Regulator) to have been personally culpable in respect of a breach of any of the Conduct Rules or Senior Manager Conduct Rules (SC1–4); or (iii) can be shown (by the Regulator) to have breached the Duty of Responsibility – that is, that he or she failed to take reasonable steps to prevent the relevant contravention occurring (or continuing) within their area of responsibility.

As a practical matter (and as alluded to earlier), it remains to be seen to what extent (if at all) the Duty of Responsibility is considered by the Regulator to differ from SC2 – whether in technical terms or relative ease of enforcement.

In theory (at least), an in-scope NED could also be criminally liable under the new offence relating to a decision causing the financial institution to fail.[65]

As discussed earlier, the Regulator can pursue Notified NEDs who can be shown to have been personally culpable in respect of a breach of any of Conduct Rules 1–5 (inclusive) or Senior Manager Conduct Rule 4.

The table below consolidates relevant PRA (*see* blue *text*) and FCA (*see* red *text*) rules/commentary/guidance relating to the Senior Manager Conduct Rules and the Presumption of Responsibility – (together with the Duty of Responsibility) the most likely avenue of potential exposure for NEDs, in practice. **Significantly, and irrespective of the precise route pursued by the Regulator, it will be important for NEDs to be able to demonstrate that they took reasonable steps/behaved reasonably in the particular circumstances**. Those provisions of most obvious relevance to NEDs are highlighted in **bold**. The table also incorporates some pointers as to what may constitute 'reasonable

---

[64] Ignoring market abuse/misconduct offences for present purposes.
[65] Under section 36 of the Financial Services (Banking Reform) Act 2013.

steps', as referenced in the PRA Supervisory Statement (SS28/15) and FCA Consultation Paper CP16/26.

The table is followed by some key questions for NEDs to consider in addressing regulatory requirements and expectations, and in helping to establish 'reasonable steps/behaviour', alongside some commentary and insights.

PRA AND FCA PRONOUNCEMENTS

Senior Manager Conduct Rules (COCON 2.1, 2.2, 4.1 and 4.2)

Rule 2: You must act with due skill, care and diligence

Acting with due skill, etc as a manager

- It is important for a manager to understand the business for which they are responsible. A manager is unlikely to be an expert in all aspects of a complex financial services business. However, they should understand and inform themselves about the business sufficiently to understand the risks of its trading, credit or other business activities.

- It is important for a manager to understand the risks of expanding the business into new areas and, before approving the expansion, they should investigate and satisfy themselves, on reasonable grounds, about the risks, if any, to the business.

- Where unusually profitable business is undertaken, or where the profits are particularly volatile or the business involves funding requirements on the firm beyond those reasonably anticipated, a manager should require explanations from those who report to him. Where those explanations are implausible or unsatisfactory, they should take steps to test the veracity of those explanations.

- Where a manager is not an expert in a business area, they should consider whether they (or those with whom they work) have

---

the necessary expertise to provide an adequate explanation of issues within that business area. If not, they should seek an independent opinion from elsewhere within or outside the firm.

The following is a non-exhaustive list of examples of conduct by a manager that would be in breach of rule 2.

(1) Failing to take reasonable steps to ensure that the business of the firm for which he has responsibility:

    (a) is controlled effectively;

    (b) complies with the relevant requirements and standards of the regulatory system applicable to that area of the business; and

    (c) is conducted in such a way to ensure that any delegation of responsibilities is to an appropriate person and is overseen effectively.

(2) Failing to take reasonable steps to adequately inform themselves about the affairs of the business for which they are responsible, including:

    (a) permitting transactions without a sufficient understanding of the risks involved;

    (b) permitting expansion of the business without reasonably assessing the potential risks of that expansion;

    (c) inadequately monitoring highly profitable transactions or business practices or unusual transactions or business practices;

    (d) accepting implausible or unsatisfactory explanations from subordinates without testing the veracity of those explanations; and

    (e) failing to obtain independent, expert opinion where appropriate.

(3) Failing to take reasonable steps to maintain an appropriate level of understanding about an issue or part of the business that the manager has delegated to an individual or individuals (whether in-house or outside contractors).

SC1: You must take reasonable steps to ensure that the business of the firm for which you are responsible is controlled effectively

- An SMF manager's role and responsibilities are set out in the statement of responsibilities.

- Strategy and plans will often dictate the risk which the business is prepared to take on and high level controls will dictate how the business is to be run. If the strategy of the business is to enter high-risk areas, then the degree of control and strength of monitoring reasonably required within the business will be high. In organising the business for which they are responsible, an SMF manager should bear this in mind.

- To comply with the obligations of rule SC1, an SMF manager may find it helpful to review whether each area of the business for which they are responsible has been clearly assigned to a particular individual or individuals.

- The organisation of the business and the responsibilities of those within it should be clearly defined. Reporting lines should be clear to staff. Where staff have dual reporting lines there is a greater need to ensure that the responsibility and accountability of each individual line manager is clearly set out and understood.

- Where members of staff have particular levels of authorisation, these should be clearly set out and communicated to staff. It may be appropriate for each member of staff to have a job description of which they are aware.

- An SMF manager should take reasonable steps to satisfy themselves, on reasonable grounds, that each area of the business for which they are responsible has appropriate policies and procedures for reviewing the competence, knowledge, skills and performance of each individual member of staff.

If an individual's performance is unsatisfactory, then the relevant SMF manager should review carefully whether to allow that individual to continue in their position. In particular, if they are aware of concerns relating to the compliance with requirements and standards of the regulatory system (or internal controls) of the individual concerned, or of staff reporting to that individual, the SMF manager should take care not to give undue weight to the financial performance of the individual or group concerned when considering whether any action should be taken. An adequate investigation of the concerns should be undertaken (including, where appropriate, adherence to internal controls). The SMF manager should be satisfied, on reasonable grounds, that the investigation is appropriate, the results are accurate and that the concerns do not pose an unacceptable risk to compliance with the requirements and standards of the regulatory system.

- As part of organising the business, an SMF manager should ensure that there is an orderly transition when another SMF manager under their oversight or responsibility ceases to perform that function and someone else takes up that function. It would be appropriate for the individual vacating such a position to prepare a comprehensive set of handover notes for his successor. Those notes should, at a minimum, specify any matter that is ongoing which the successor would reasonably expect to be aware of to:

  (1) perform their function effectively;

  (2) ensure compliance with the requirements and standards of the regulatory system; and

  (3) ensure that the individual with overall responsibility for that part of the business of the firm maintains effective control.

In organising the business, an SMF manager should pay attention to any temporary vacancies which exist. They should take reasonable steps to ensure that suitable cover for responsibilities is arranged. This could include taking on temporary staff or external consultants. The SMF manager should assess the risk that is posed to compliance with the requirements and standards of the regulatory system as a result of the vacancy, and the higher the risk the greater the steps they should take to fill the vacancy. It may be appropriate to limit or suspend the activity if adequate cover for responsibilities cannot be arranged. To the extent that those vacancies are for controlled functions, they may only be filled by persons approved for that function.

- The following is a non-exhaustive list of examples of conduct that would be in breach of rule SC1.

(1) Failing to take reasonable steps to apportion responsibilities for all areas of the business under the approved person's control.

(2) Failing to take reasonable steps to apportion responsibilities clearly among those to whom responsibilities have been delegated, which includes establishing confusing or uncertain:

    (a) reporting lines;or

    (b) authorisation levels; or

    (c) job descriptions and responsibilities.

(3) In the case of a manager who is responsible for dealing with the apportionment of responsibilities, failing to take reasonable care to maintain a clear and appropriate apportionment of responsibilities, including:

    (a) failing to review regularly the responsibilities which have been apportioned; and

    (b) failing to act where that review shows that those responsibilities have not been clearly apportioned.

(4) Failing to take reasonable steps to ensure that suitable individuals are responsible for those aspects of the business under the control of the individual performing a senior management function, including the following:

    (a) failing to review the competence, knowledge, skills and performance of staff to assess their suitability to fulfil their duties, despite evidence that their performance is unacceptable;

    (b) giving undue weight to financial performance when considering the suitability or continuing suitability of an individual for a particular role; and

(c) allowing managerial vacancies which put compliance with the requirements and standards of the regulatory system at risk to remain, without arranging suitable cover for the responsibilities.

SC2: You must take reasonable steps to ensure that the business of the firm for which you are responsible complies with the relevant requirements and standards of the regulatory system

- An SMF manager must take reasonable steps both to ensure his firm's compliance with the relevant requirements and standards of the regulatory system and to ensure that all staff are aware of the need for compliance.

- An SMF manager need not themself put in place the systems of control for the business, unless it is within their role and responsibilities. However, they should take reasonable steps to ensure that the business for which they are responsible has operating procedures and systems with well-defined steps for complying with the detail of relevant requirements and standards of the regulatory system and for ensuring that the business is run prudently. The nature and extent of the systems of control that are required will depend upon the relevant requirements and standards of the regulatory system, and the nature, scale and complexity of the business.

- Where an SMF manager becomes aware of actual or suspected problems that involve possible breaches of relevant requirements and standards of the regulatory system falling within their area of responsibility, they should take reasonable steps to ensure that they are dealt with in a timely and appropriate manner. This may involve an adequate investigation to find out whether any systems or procedures have failed and why. They may need to obtain expert opinion on the adequacy and efficacy of the systems and procedures.

- If an issue raises questions of law or interpretation, an SMF manager may need to take legal advice. If appropriate legal expertise is not available in-house, they may need to consider appointing an appropriate external adviser.

- Where independent reviews of systems and procedures have been undertaken and result in recommendations for improvement, the SMF manager responsible for that business area should ensure that, unless there are good reasons not to, any reasonable recommendations are implemented in a timely manner. What is reasonable will depend on the nature of the issue to be addressed and the cost of the improvement. It will be reasonable for the SMF manager to carry out a cost benefit analysis when assessing whether the recommendations are reasonable.

- The following is a non-exhaustive list of examples of conduct that would be in breach of rule SC2.

  (1) Failing to take reasonable steps to implement (either personally or through a compliance department or other departments) adequate and appropriate systems of control to comply with the relevant requirements and standards of the regulatory system for the activities of the firm.

  (2) Failing to take reasonable steps to monitor (either personally or through a compliance department or other departments) compliance with the relevant requirements and standards of the regulatory system for the activities of the firm in question.

  (3) Failing to take reasonable steps to inform themselves adequately about the reason why significant breaches (suspected or actual) of the relevant requirements and standards of the regulatory system for the activities of the firm in question may have arisen (taking account of the systems and procedures in place). This would include failing to investigate whether systems or procedures may have failed and failing to obtain expert opinion on the adequacy of the systems and procedures where appropriate.

  (4) Failing to take reasonable steps to ensure that procedures and systems of control are reviewed and, if appropriate, improved, following the identification of significant breaches (suspected or actual) of the relevant requirements and

standards of the regulatory system relating to the activities of the firm including:

(a) unreasonably failing to implement recommendations for improvements in systems and procedures; and

(b) unreasonably failing to implement recommendations for improvements to systems and procedures in a timely manner.

(5) For a manager with responsibility for overseeing the establishment and maintenance of appropriate systems and controls or the apportionment of responsibilities, any failure to take reasonable care, to ensure that these obligations are discharged effectively.

(6) For a proprietary trader, failing to maintain and comply with appropriate systems and controls in relation to that activity.

(7) For a money laundering reporting officer, failing to discharge the responsibilities imposed on them by the firm for oversight of its compliance with the FCA's rules on systems and controls against money laundering.

(8) For an SMF manager who is responsible for the compliance function, failing to ensure that:

(a) the compliance function has the necessary authority, resources, expertise and access to all relevant information; or

(b) a compliance officer is appointed and is responsible for the compliance function and for any reporting as to compliance; or

(c) the persons involved in the compliance functions are not involved in the performance of services or activities they monitor; or

(d) the method of determining the remuneration of the persons involved in the compliance function does not compromise their objectivity; or

(e) the method of determining the remuneration complies, where applicable, with the Remuneration Code.

SC3: You must take reasonable steps to ensure that any delegation of your responsibilities is to an appropriate person and that you oversee the discharge of the delegated responsibility effectively

- An SMF manager may delegate the investigation, resolution or management of an issue or authority for dealing with a part of the business to individuals who report to them or to others.

- An SMF manager should have reasonable grounds for believing that the delegate has the competence, knowledge, skill and time to deal with the issue. For instance, if the compliance department only has sufficient resources to deal with day-to-day issues, it would be unreasonable to delegate to it the resolution of a complex or unusual issue without ensuring it had sufficient capacity to deal with the matter adequately.

- The FCA recognises that an SMF manager will have to exercise their own judgement in deciding how issues are dealt with and sometimes that judgement will, with the benefit of hindsight, be shown to have been wrong. The SMF manager will not be in breach of rule SC3 in COCON 2.2.3R unless they fail to exercise due and reasonable consideration before they delegate the resolution of an issue or authority for dealing with a part of the business and fail to reach a reasonable conclusion. If they are in doubt about how to deal with an issue or the seriousness of a particular compliance problem, then, although they cannot delegate to the FCA the responsibility for dealing with the problem or issue, they can speak to the FCA to discuss his approach.

- An SMF manager will not always manage the business on a day-to-day basis themselves. The extent to which they do so will depend on a number of factors, including the nature, scale and complexity of the business and their position within it. The larger and more complex the business, the greater the need for clear and effective delegation and reporting lines, which may involve documenting the scope of that delegation and the reporting lines in writing. The FCA will look to the SMF manager to take reasonable steps to ensure that systems are in place to ensure that issues are being addressed at the appropriate level. When issues come to their attention, they should deal with them in an appropriate way.

Delegating the authority for dealing with an issue or a part of the business to an individual or individuals (whether in-house or outside contractors) without reasonable grounds for believing that the delegate had the necessary capacity, competence, knowledge, seniority or skill to deal with the issue or to take authority for dealing with part of the business indicates a failure to comply with rule SC3 in COCON 2.2.3R.

Although an SMF manager may delegate the resolution of an issue, or authority for dealing with a part of the business, they cannot delegate responsibility for it. It is that person's responsibility to ensure that they receive reports on progress and question those reports where appropriate. For instance, if progress appears to be slow or if the issue is not being resolved satisfactorily, then the SMF manager may need to challenge the explanations they receive and, take action personally to resolve the problem. This may include increasing the resource applied to it, reassigning the resolution internally or obtaining external advice or assistance. Where an issue raises significant concerns, an SMF manager should act clearly and decisively. If appropriate, this may be by suspending members of staff or relieving them of all or part of their responsibilities.

The following is a non-exhaustive list of examples of conduct that would be in breach of rule SC3.

(1) Failing to take reasonable steps to maintain an appropriate level of understanding about an issue or part of the business that he has delegated to an individual(s) (whether in-house or outside contractors) including:

(a) disregarding an issue or part of the business once it has been delegated;

(b) failing to require adequate reports once the resolution of an issue or management of part of the business has been delegated; and

(c) accepting implausible or unsatisfactory explanations from delegates without testing their accuracy.

(2) Failing to supervise and monitor adequately the individual(s) (whether in-house or outside contractors) to whom responsibility for dealing with an issue or authority for dealing with a part of the business has been delegated including any failure to:

(a) take personal action where progress is unreasonably slow, or where implausible or unsatisfactory explanations are provided; or

(b) review the performance of an outside contractor in connection with the delegated issue or business.

- In determining whether or not the conduct of an SMF manager complies with rule SC3 in COCON 2.2.3R, the factors which the FCA would expect to take into account include:

(1) the competence, knowledge or seniority of the delegate; and

(2) the past performance and record of the delegate.

SC4: You must disclose appropriately any information of which the FCA or PRA would reasonably expect notice

- For the purpose of rule SC4, regulators in addition to the FCA and the PRA are those which have recognised jurisdiction in relation to activities to which COCON applies and have a power to call for information from the relevant person in connection with their function or the business for which they are responsible. This may include an exchange or an overseas regulator.

- SC4 applies to an SMF manager in addition to rule 3 in COCON 2.1.3R. Although the rules have some overlap, they are different. Rule 3 normally relates to responses from individuals to requests from the regulator, whereas rule SC4 imposes a duty on SMF managers to disclose appropriately any information of which the appropriate regulator would reasonably expect, including making a disclosure in the absence of any request or enquiry from the appropriate regulator. An SMF manager is likely to have access to greater amounts of information of potential regulatory importance and to have the expertise to recognise when this may be something of which the appropriate regulator would reasonably expect notice.

- Where a person is responsible within the firm (individually or with other SMF managers) for reporting matters to the regulator, failing promptly to inform the regulator concerned of information of which they are aware and which it would be reasonable to assume would be of material significance to the regulator concerned, whether in response to questions or otherwise, constitutes a breach of rule SC4 in COCON 2.2.4R.

- If an SMF manager comes across a piece of information that is something in relation to which they think the FCA or PRA could reasonably expect notice, they should determine whether that information falls within the scope of their responsibilities (for an SMF manager, by virtue of that person's statement of responsibilities). If it does, then they should ensure that, if it is otherwise appropriate to do so, it is disclosed to the appropriate regulator. If it does not fall within the scope of their responsibilities then, in the absence of any reason to the contrary, they might reasonably assume that its disclosure to the appropriate regulator was being dealt with by the SMF manager with responsibility for dealing with information of that nature. If an SMF manager was not sure that the matter was being dealt with by another SMF manager, or if they were not sure whether this was in their area or not, the FCA would expect them to make enquiries to inform themselves, rather than disregard the matter.

- In determining whether or not a person's conduct complies with rule SC4 in COCON 2.2.4R, the factors which the FCA would expect to take into account include:

  (1) whether it would be reasonable for the individual to assume that the information would be of material significance to the regulator concerned;

  (2) whether the information related to the individual themselves or to their firm; and

(3) whether any decision not to report the matter was taken after reasonable enquiry and analysis of the situation.

Practical pointers on 'reasonable steps'

The steps that a Senior Manager should take ... are such steps as would have been taken by a competent Senior Manager at that time in that specific individual's position with that individual's role and responsibilities in all the existing circumstances. Senior Managers, when considering what steps to take, should also have regard to their existing statutory, common law and equitable obligations, including those set out in the Companies Act 2006, the Conduct Rules, the UK Corporate Governance Code, and the Model Code.[66]

Section 66B(5)(d) involves the PRA assessing (a) the steps that the specific Senior Manager actually took, against (b) such steps as the PRA considers that a Senior Manager, in that position, could reasonably have been expected to take to avoid the contravention occurring (or continuing). The PRA's expectations of the steps in (b) will necessarily depend on the circumstances as they existed at the time. It is not the PRA's intention to apply standards retrospectively or with the benefit of hindsight. However, examples of the considerations that the PRA may consider in forming its view of (b) can include:

- the size, scale and complexity of the firm;
- what the Senior Manager actually knew, or a Senior Manager in that position ought to have known (taking into account, among other factors, the length of time they have been in the role and handover arrangements to those new in a role);
- what expertise and competence the Senior Manager had, or ought to have possessed, at the time to perform his or her specific Senior Management Function;

---

[66] Paragraphs 5.1, 5.5 and 5.6 FCA: CP 15/9, "Strengthening Accountability in Banking: A New Regulatory Framework for Individuals – Feedback on FCA CP14/13/PRA CP14/14 and Consultation on Additional Guidance", March 2015.

- what steps the Senior Manager could have taken, considering what alternative actions might have been open to the Senior Manager at the time and the timeliness within which he or she could have acted;

- the actual responsibilities of that Senior Manager and the relationship between those responsibilities and the responsibilities of other Senior Managers in the firm (including in relation to any joint responsibilities or matrix-management structures);

- whether the Senior Manager delegated any functions, taking into account that any such delegation should be appropriately arranged, managed and monitored; and

- the overall circumstances and environment at the firm and more widely, in which such a Senior Manager was operating at the time. For example, where a Senior Manager was subject to competing priorities, the PRA may consider whether the way in which he or she prioritised them was informed by an appropriate risk assessment.

In relation to (a) and the steps that a Senior Manager actually took to avoid the contravention occurring or continuing, examples of the steps that may be considered to be reasonable actions, depending on the circumstances, could include:

- pre-emptive actions to prevent a breach occurring, including any initial reviews of the business or business area on taking up a Senior Manager function;

- implementing, policing and reviewing appropriate policies and procedures;

- awareness of relevant requirements and standards of the regulatory system;

- investigations or reviews of the Senior Manager's area of responsibilities;

- where a breach is continuing, any response taken to that breach;

- structuring and control of day-to-day operations, including ensuring any delegations are managed and reviewed appropriately. This includes in relation to any 'matrix-management' arrangements;

- obtaining appropriate internal management information, and critically interrogating and monitoring that information;
- raising issues, reviewing issues, and following them up with relevant staff, committees and boards;
- seeking and obtaining appropriate expert advice or assurance, whether internal or external;
- ensuring that the firm and/or relevant area has adequate resources, and that these are appropriately deployed, including for risk and control functions; and
- awareness of relevant external developments, including key risks.

Evidence that the PRA might seek to obtain in respect of these kinds of matters could include:

- board and board committee minutes;
- minutes of other internal meetings;
- Statements of Responsibilities and Responsibilities Maps;
- organisation charts and information on reporting lines;
- any other internal materials, for example, emails or telephone recordings; and
- regulatory correspondence and interviews.

An SMF manager is guilty of misconduct further to section 66A(5) of the Act where:

- there has been (or continued to be) a contravention of a relevant requirement by the SMF manager's firm;
- at the time of the contravention, the SMF manager was responsible for the management of any of the firm's activities in relation to which the contravention occurred;
- in a contested case, the FCA establishes points (1) and (2), above, in any proceedings before the RDC, a court or a tribunal, with the SMF manager as a party to the action; and

- the SMF manager does not satisfy the FCA that they had taken such steps as a person in their position could reasonably be expected to take to avoid the contravention by the firm occurring (or continuing) ...[67]

When determining, for the purposes of section 66A(5) of the Act, whether an SMF manager was responsible for the management of any of the firm's activities in relation to which a contravention of a relevant requirement by the firm occurred, the FCA will consider the full circumstances of each case.

A list of considerations that may be relevant for this purpose is set out below. This list is not exhaustive: there may be other considerations, not listed, that are relevant.

- The SMF manager's statement of responsibilities, including whether the SMF manager was performing an executive or non-executive role.
- The firm's management responsibilities map.
- How the firm operated, and how responsibilities were allocated in the firm in practice.
- The SMF manager's actual role and responsibilities in the firm, to be determined by reference to, among other things, the minutes of meetings, emails, interviews, telephone recordings and organisational charts.
- The relationship between the SMF manager's responsibilities and the responsibilities of other SMF managers in the firm.

Under section 66A(5)(d) of the Act, such steps as a person in the position of the SMF manager could reasonably be expected to take to avoid the firm's contravention of a relevant requirement occurring (or continuing) are:

(1) such steps as a competent SMF manager would have taken;

(2) at that time;

---

[67] Draft Handbook text DEPP 6.2.9-AG: CP 15/9, "Strengthening Accountability in Banking: A New Regulatory Framework for Individuals – Feedback on FCA CP14/13/PRA CP14/14 and Consultation on Additional Guidance", March 2015.

(3) in that specific individual's position;

(4) with that individual's role and responsibilities;

(5) in all the existing circumstances.

When determining whether or not an SMF manager satisfies the FCA under section 66A(5)(d) of the Act, that they had taken such steps as a person in their position could reasonably be expected to take to avoid the contravention of a relevant requirement by the firm occurring (or continuing), additional considerations to which the FCA would expect to have regard include, but are not limited to:

(1) the role and responsibilities of the SMF manager;

(2) whether the SMF manager exercised reasonable care when considering the information available to them;

(3) whether the SMF manager reached a reasonable conclusion on which to act;

(4) the nature, scale and complexity of the firm's business;

(5) the knowledge the SMF manager had, or should have had, of regulatory concerns, if any, relating to their role and responsibilities;

(6) whether the SMF manager, where they were aware of, or should have been aware of, actual or suspected issues where these involved possible breaches by their firm of relevant requirements relating to their role and responsibilities, took reasonable steps to ensure that they were dealt with in a timely and appropriate manner;

(7) whether the SMF manager acted in accordance with their statutory, common law and other legal obligations, including, but not limited to, the (Senior Manager) Conduct Rules (and other relevant rules) set out in the FCA Handbook, those set out in the Companies Act 2006, the Handbook (including COCON), and, if the firm was listed on the London Stock Exchange, the UK Corporate Governance Code and related guidance;

(8) whether the SMF manager took reasonable steps to ensure that any delegation of their responsibilities, where this was itself reasonable, was to an appropriate person, with the necessary

capacity, competence, knowledge, seniority or skill, and whether they took reasonable steps to oversee the discharge of the delegated responsibility effectively;

(9) whether the SMF manager took reasonable steps to ensure that the reporting lines, whether in the UK or overseas, in relation to the firm's activities for which they were responsible, were clear to staff and operated effectively;

(10) whether the SMF manager took reasonable steps to satisfy themselves, on reasonable grounds, that, for the activities for which they were responsible, the firm had appropriate policies and procedures for reviewing the competence, knowledge, skills and performance of each individual member of staff, to assess their suitability to fulfil their duties;

(11) whether the SMF manager took reasonable steps to assess, on taking up each of their responsibilities, and monitor, where this was reasonable, the governance, operational and risk management arrangements in place for the firm's activities for which they were responsible (including, where appropriate, corroborating, challenging, and considering the wider implications of the information available to them), and whether they took reasonable steps to deal with any actual or suspected issues identified as a result in a timely and appropriate manner;

(12) whether the SMF manager took reasonable steps to ensure an orderly transition when another SMF manager under their oversight or responsibility was replaced in the performance of that function by someone else;

(13) whether the SMF manager took reasonable steps to ensure an orderly transition when they were replaced in the performance of their function by someone else;

(14) whether the SMF manager took reasonable steps to understand and inform themselves about the firm's activities in relation to which they were responsible, including, but not limited to, whether they:

(a) permitted the expansion or restructuring of the business without reasonably assessing the potential risks;

(b) inadequately monitored highly profitable transactions, business practices, unusual transactions or individuals who contributed significantly to the profitability of a business area or who had significant influence over the operation of a business area;

(c) failed to obtain independent, expert opinion where appropriate from within or outside the firm;

(d) failed to seek an adequate explanation of issues within a business area, whether from people within that business area, or elsewhere within or outside the firm, if they were not an expert in that area;

(e) failed to maintain an appropriate level of understanding about an issue or a responsibility that they delegated to an individual or individuals;

(15) whether the SMF manager took reasonable steps to ensure that where they were involved in a collective decision affecting the firm's activities for which they were responsible, where it was reasonable for the decision to be taken collectively, they informed themselves of the relevant matters before taking part in the decision, and exercised reasonable care, skill and diligence in contributing to the decision;

(16) whether the SMF manager took reasonable steps to follow the firm's procedures, where this was itself appropriate;

(17) how long the SMF manager had been in role with their responsibilities and whether there was an orderly transition and handover when they took up the role and responsibilities; and

(18) whether the SMF manager took reasonable steps to implement (either personally or through a compliance department or other departments) adequate and appropriate systems and controls to comply with the relevant requirements and standards of the regulatory system for the activities of the firm.

KEY QUESTIONS TO CONSIDER

The Regulator's view of NEDs

Questions

- Do I understand how the Regulator views the role and key responsibilities of NEDs?
- Do I appreciate that I am viewed as an essential 'check and balance', to help ensure that the Executive is held to account?
- Do I appreciate the importance of demonstrable challenge to the Executive?
- Do I understand the overriding importance to the Regulator of clients' interests and market integrity?

Comments

NEDs are regarded as a fundamental safeguard within a firm's governance framework – in holding the Executive to account and also in ensuring that clients' interests are afforded due consideration and weight.

Reasonable steps

Questions

In any given situation, a NED might usefully ask:

- What more could I reasonably have been expected to do in the circumstances?
- What could I reasonably be criticised for having not done?

Comments

Following a regulatory breach by a firm, a NED considered responsible for the firm's activities in respect of which the contravention occurred will need to be in a position to demonstrate, if challenged by the Regulator under the Duty of Responsibility, that he or she has taken such reasonable steps as would have been taken by a competent NED at that time in that specific individual's position. Similarly, a NED being pursued under the (Senior Manager) Conduct Rules must also, in effect, be able to evidence 'reasonable steps'.

The need for a NED to be able to evidence 'reasonable steps' exists despite the fact that, technically, the burden of proof falls on the Regulator. In essence, this is a reflection of the fact that as soon as an allegation is made by the Regulator, the buck reflectively passes to the NED. If the NED cannot establish 'reasonable steps', the Regulator's case is effectively made out – that is, unless and until it is challenged before the Upper Tribunal (not a course that every such NED will wish to pursue).

Reasonable steps will include both pre-emptive and remedial actions.

When considering what constitutes 'reasonable steps', the Regulator will have regard to all the circumstances applicable, including (without limitation): the NED's responsibilities; whether the NED exercised reasonable care and reached reasonable conclusions; what knowledge and expertise the NED possessed (or should have possessed) at the time; and relevant regulatory requirements.

External assurance/input can often serve a useful purpose in this regard (see 'Use of experts' below).

Importance of demonstrability

Recent experience suggests that senior individuals who are unable to corroborate their account with demonstrable evidence are unlikely to be able to satisfy the Regulator of the reasonableness of their conduct (and hence persuade the Regulator to drop any proposed enforcement action). In other words, the Regulator may well doubt whether an event really happened if there is no supporting (ideally, contemporaneous) documentary evidence. An unfair working presumption perhaps, but reality nonetheless.

By way of example, the Regulator will expect to see NED challenge and consideration of clients' interests, risk and compliance feature sufficiently prominently in relevant board/committee minutes. In practice, the Regulator is unlikely to accept that clients' interests were appropriately discussed without contemporaneous documentary evidence to support such contention.

Where possible, relevant matters would be evidenced through meeting minutes,[68] file notes and other forms of contemporaneous documentary correspondence/records. While this does not of course mean that every last piece of dialogue, deliberation and thought process must be studiously recorded, it nevertheless requires an ongoing awareness of those matters or issues most likely (or with greatest potential) to attract subsequent regulatory scrutiny. As an informal rule of thumb, a NED might usefully consider whether the matter at hand has real potential to 'come back to bite' them. In many cases, this will be reasonably self-evident – one way or the other. Chapter 9 elaborates further on the topic of record-keeping.

NEDs should consider whether any dissenting views have been recorded appropriately.

Standard of care

The standard of care, skill and diligence that the Regulator would expect from a NED is the care, skill and diligence that would be exercised by a reasonably diligent person with: (i) the general knowledge and experience that may reasonably be expected of a person carrying out the functions carried out by the NED in relation to the firm; and (ii) the general knowledge, skill and experience that the NED possesses.

Understanding/challenge/decision-making

Questions

- Could I comfortably summarise the firm's strategy, business model, product lines and customer base?
- Similarly, could I readily articulate the key risks faced by the firm and the attendant controls?
- In all honesty, do I consider that I possess the necessary skills and experience to carry out my agreed responsibilities?

---

[68] Many financial institutions have recently revisited the manner in which formal minutes are recorded – to ensure (amongst other things) that they are sufficiently balanced, comprehensive and reflective of all challenge.

- Have I gained a sufficient inherent understanding of the business in order for me to properly scrutinise the performance of management and deliver informed challenge?

- Am I comfortable that I receive an appropriate level of management information to enable me to perform my challenge and oversight role?

- Could I demonstrate to the Regulator, in respect of significant decisions taken, that all options available were discussed and duly considered? Would this be borne out in the relevant board or committee minutes?

- Am I confident that the relevant board or committee minutes would appropriately reflect the due consideration of clients' interests and conduct risk?

- Do I critically review management information provided and raise any 'red flags' or issues with the board/committee, as appropriate? Could I explain to the Regulator how these are being (or have been) addressed and what follow-up reporting is provided?

- Am I alert to potentially troubling emerging trends/themes?

- Am I comfortable that any questions posed or challenges raised receive satisfactory responses?

Operating procedures

- Do I understand (and could I articulate at a high level) what operating procedures and systems have been implemented to ensure compliance with these key regulatory requirements?

- Is a watching brief kept on such procedures and systems to ensure that they remain fit for purpose? In practice, what does this entail? For example, what form(s) of assurance are received, from whom and how regularly?

- Are there any legacy issues which remain unresolved? Is there any obvious scope for improvement?

Comments

Strategy and business model

NEDs will be expected to have a sound understanding of the firm's strategy, business model, customers and products. Without such an appreciation, it follows that a NED would be ill-equipped to assess inherent risks and provide insightful challenge to the Executive on all aspects of the business, including culture.

For example, in the context of strategic business decisions, NEDs would be expected to be challenging the Executive to ensure that the potential impact on clients and their fair treatment are duly considered from the very outset.

A NED's failure to understand (and be able to articulate at a high level) the key risks faced by the firm and the associated controls is likely to serve as a 'red flag' for the Regulator.

Management information

During the normal course of business, NEDs should perform their oversight role by scrutinising the management information provided. It is essential that the management information is of the requisite quality to enable NEDs to properly perform their functions. Any concerns around the quality of management information received should be raised and satisfactorily resolved. Importantly, management information must strike an appropriate balance: it should not be unwieldy and over-detailed; however, at the same time, it should be sufficiently instructive to enable a NED to obtain the necessary degree of visibility and oversight, and to make well-informed decisions.

For example, reports may consistently indicate that there are no issues to be addressed. In such circumstances, NEDs might question whether the management information provided is sufficient – in other words, is it 'too good to be true'?

Similarly, NEDs should remain alert to, and actively challenge, any potentially problematic emerging themes or trends that may be indicative of wider systemic issues. By way of illustrative example:

- Recurrent non-completion of mandatory training.

- Repeated breaches of internal policies and procedures (such as personal account (PA) dealing rules).

- Recurrent regulatory compliance issues (for instance, trade reporting errors; failure to adhere to internal policies, such as complaints handling; or CASS rule breaches).

- Frequent IT/systems issues.

- Recurrent instances of non-escalation of important issues.

- Repeated breach of Service Level Agreements by third parties.

- Repeated deadlines missed in the context of important projects.

Risk management

Questions

- Do I have a sufficiently strong grasp of the risk management framework – in particular, its design, operational effectiveness and any specific weaknesses? Could I articulate this framework at an interview with the Regulator?

- Do I properly understand (and could I readily summarise) both the compliance and operational risk assessment process(es)?

- More specifically, could I comfortably describe the firm's conduct risk management framework, risk appetite and tolerance, and how 'conduct risk' is defined within my firm?

- Are the risk management framework and controls periodically reviewed to ensure that they remain fit for purpose? Do I have the requisite visibility over the outputs of such reviews? Is there obvious room for improvement?

- Could I explain how the 3 Lines of Defence model operates within the firm and where I fit in?

- Do I understand (in broad terms) how my firm's ICAAP is compiled?

- Could I explain what purpose(s) the ICAAP serves?

- Can I articulate the firm's risk appetite/tolerance, and how the firm ensures that it continues to operate within these parameters? Do I understand what 'checks and balances' exist to ensure that these parameters are respected?

Operational risk

- Do I really understand the operational risks inherent in the business and emanating from the firm's business model and strategy, and the associated systems of control? Are these risks and controls periodically assessed? How and by whom?
- Does the management information provided actually facilitate such an assessment?
- Do I have confidence in, and sufficient visibility over, the Operational Risk function?
- Do I really understand how the business makes its money and the drivers of its primary source(s) of revenue?

Risk awareness

- Am I consciously alert to red flags – for example, unusual transactions or practices; worrying trends; inordinately profitable products; unsatisfactory or implausible explanations from delegates or third party associates?
- Do I challenge and ask searching questions, where necessary – for example, around seemingly implausible explanations?

Comments

The Regulator expects the firm's strategy to be supported by a statement of risk appetite which can be readily understood by the entire organisation. The board should both take ownership of such a statement and ensure that it is actively used when assessing risks and considering key business decisions.

As a matter of course, the Regulator will expect NEDs to have a sound understanding of the firm's risk management framework, as well as its financial controls and remuneration model(s). These are topics frequently raised at regulatory interviews with NEDs.

It will be important for an incoming NED to quickly get up to speed with the firm's overall risk and control environment; and form an initial assessment as to whether any obvious/significant issues exist. In respect of any legacy risk issues, NEDs should obtain assurance that these have been satisfactorily resolved.

A failure to display a sound understanding of the firm's risk management framework may serve as a red flag for the Regulator. The preparation of simple schematics illustrating the risk management framework may be a helpful tool for NEDs. Such schematics could serve a number of purposes, such as ensuring clarity, and identifying gaps, anomalies or issues that need to be addressed. They might also serve as useful papers to be furnished to the Regulator (if appropriate) during a supervisory visit.

3 Lines of Defence model

NEDs should be able to describe the firm's 3 Lines of Defence risk management model, and (at a high level) how it operates in practice.

Risk awareness

NEDs should continually be alert to any potential red flag issues, or any emerging themes, trends or patterns which may be viewed as indicative of wider systemic concerns. By way of example, recurrences of the following types of issue/incident might well serve as red flags:

- repeated contraventions by a member of staff of internal policies or procedures;
- repeated trade reporting errors;
- especially high staff turnover in certain teams or departments;
- poor mandatory training attendance;
- repeated/significant limit breaches;
- frequently missed deadlines on key projects;
- consistently sub-standard service from outsourcees;
- troubling staff survey results;
- high customer complaint rates; and
- poor exit interview feedback;

Governance

Questions

- Do I have a sufficiently strong grasp of the governance framework – in particular, its design, operational effectiveness and any specific weaknesses? Could I articulate this framework at an interview with the Regulator?

- Am I clear as to my role(s) within the governance framework and how/where I fit into the grand scheme?

- Is the governance framework periodically reviewed to ensure that it remains fit for purpose? If so, by whom and how frequently? Do I have the requisite visibility over the outputs of such reviews?

- Could I explain how the 3 Lines of Defence model operates within the firm and where I reside?

- Are there too many committees, with overlapping responsibilities, within the governance framework?

- Are there any obvious gaps?

- Are committees appropriately constituted?

- Are all Terms of Reference clear, with no potential for confusion/ overlap?

- Could I readily explain (at a high level) the purpose and function of each key committee within the governance framework?

- Are issues being dealt with at the right levels within the governance framework?

- Is there obvious room for improvement?

Oversight and escalation

- Am I comfortable that I would have sufficient visibility over any significant issues or incidents arising within the firm? Can I point to recent examples?

- Can I articulate what formal escalation channels exist? Am I confident that these are widely known and observed?

- When was the last time that an issue was escalated to the board or a committee on which I sit?

Comments

Effective organisation and governance

Governance is (and will likely remain) a key area of focus for the Regulator. Accordingly, it will be important for NEDs to be able to describe (and display a sound understanding of) the firm's governance framework.

NEDs must seek to ensure that the business is being run in a manner consistent with the firm's risk appetite and tolerance.

The preparation and maintenance of simple schematics illustrating both reporting lines and the allocation of responsibility could be a helpful tool for NEDs. Such schematics could serve a number of purposes, such as ensuring clarity, and identifying gaps, anomalies or issues that need to be addressed. They might also serve as useful papers to be furnished to the Regulator (if appropriate) during a supervisory visit.

Delegation

Questions

- Am I satisfied that appropriate due diligence was undertaken prior to the delegation of a material issue, project or aspect of the business?
- When delegating, is sufficient demonstrable thought given to the delegate's capacity, expertise and experience to perform the delegated task(s)?
- How comfortable would I feel in articulating (and demonstrating) this to the Regulator?
- Am I satisfied that the firm has retained an appropriate understanding of any business or services delegated?
- What ongoing oversight is maintained over delegates and delegated issues/business? Is this effective or is there room for improvement? How is this evidenced?

Comments

Delegation of functions poses obvious risks to a Senior Manager's effective control of the business for which he or she is responsible.

In respect of delegation by the board, the Regulator will expect that any reserved matters are clearly specified, and that the manner in which executive management must report and escalate matters is well understood and appropriately documented.

In respect of any delegation by a Senior Manager, the Regulator will expect that the delegate was selected following appropriate consideration and that the Senior Manager maintains an appropriate degree of effective oversight of the delegated functions.

An ill-considered delegation, for example, to an individual at an inappropriate level may cause the Regulator to question a Senior Manager's exercise of responsibility.

Senior Managers should approach delegation with the understanding that although they may delegate the handling of a particular issue or aspect of the business, they cannot delegate their responsibility for it. They must therefore be comfortable that they receive sufficient periodic information in order to supervise the delegation effectively and to retain an adequate understanding of the services delegated.

A pre-delegation protocol, incorporating a practical checklist, might usefully be considered (if one does not already exist). Such a protocol might cover (amongst other things):

- the delegate's specifically relevant credentials and expertise, and proven track record;
- the delegate's capacity and capability for the role in question;
- (in respect of an external delegation) the form of agreement in place with the delegate – which would ordinarily be expected to include (amongst other things): provisions affording the delegating firm supervision/monitoring rights; periodic reporting/management information requirements; appropriate termination rights; service level standards; and resource commitment; and

- (in respect of an internal delegation) an agreed reporting schedule providing for periodic reporting/management information; periodic catch-up meetings; and scheduled performance review sessions.

NED Regulatory Awareness

Questions

- Do I fully appreciate the key regulatory requirements (and expectations) relevant to my firm? For example, am I familiar with any recently issued thematic reports, relevant to the firm's business?
- Could I comfortably articulate these to the Regulator, if required?
- Am I confident that any material regulatory developments are drawn to my attention in a timely manner?
- Are regulatory enforcement notices against other firms or individuals and other regulatory pronouncements (such as thematic reports) being actively monitored – to assess whether there is any potential 'read-across' onto (or lessons to be learned within) our business?
- Do I receive periodic (and meaningful) refresher training? When was my last training session?
- Do I have knowledge gaps, which need to be plugged?

Comments

NEDs are expected to have a strong grasp of (and be able to articulate) the regulatory environment in which they are operating. Periodic refresher training and awareness sessions (in particular, on regulatory hot topics) are now widely regarded as essential.

NEDs should ensure that they: are kept abreast (in a timely manner) of pertinent regulatory developments; and have sufficient knowledge and expertise to help contextualise and identify any areas of concern.

NEDs should also ensure that the firm is actively monitoring regulatory developments and enforcement actions against other firms or individuals – to assess whether there is any potential application or read-across onto (or lessons to be learned within) the firm's own business.

Use of experts

Questions

- Do I appreciate the value in obtaining an independent expert opinion, where appropriate – for example, where this may help to provide a further layer of (objective and professional) assurance, offer some important industry perspective or help to validate an approach taken?
- Do the potential benefits outweigh the costs?
- If ever challenged by the Regulator, would I regret not having suggested or sought such expert guidance?

Comments

Where appropriate, NEDs should consider whether it would be desirable to enlist the services of external specialists – for example, to assist with the remediation of identified issues; to help support/validate a particular stance adopted; to provide a degree of independent assurance; and/or to assist with the implementation of specific projects.

NEDs might prudently assume that they may be challenged on why independent advice or assistance was not sought in a specific scenario. Whilst this is not a firm requirement as such, it will be important for a NED to have a credible response, and to be able to justify why external input was not considered necessary in the circumstances.

Pre-emptive measures and reactivity

Questions

- Where an issue arises, am I confident that the firm would respond decisively and robustly (and be seen to respond as such)?
- In respect of any materialised breaches, am I able to explain to the Regulator the remedial action taken?
- Would I be inclined to challenge and ask searching questions – for example, around provisional conclusions reached or assurances provided? Would I be able to evidence this, if challenged?

Comments

Robust responsiveness

Following an identified breach, NEDs must be able to demonstrate that timely, credible and effective action was taken, and that all viable responses were duly considered and challenged – and, if necessary, be able to readily justify the chosen remedial course. The Regulator would also expect a NED to proactively investigate (and discover) the underlying reason(s) (root causes) of any significant compliance breach. Any lessons to be learned should also be expressly considered.

NEDs must ensure that they receive adequate management information regarding the implementation and effectiveness of the responsive/remedial measures undertaken, so that progress can be actively monitored and, if necessary, challenged.

NEDs should appreciate that their firm's response to an identified breach is likely to serve as a key cultural indicator for the Regulator.[69] It is therefore essential that any such response is seen to be sufficiently robust and can be readily evidenced. NEDs can play an important role here.

Orderly transitions

Questions

- Am I sufficiently familiar with the orderly transition procedures; and do I understand my responsibilities in this regard?

Comments

Transitional periods present particular risks to firms and are an obvious area of potential challenge.

Where appropriate, NEDs should be comfortable that there are appropriate handover procedures in place, and that there are no gaps in responsibility or expertise.

---

[69] See further Chapter 6.

Compliance function

Questions

For Senior Managers responsible for the Compliance function:

- Am I comfortable that the Compliance function has the necessary authority, resources, expertise and access to relevant management information?

- Does the Compliance Officer have clear reporting lines for updating and escalating compliance issues to the board?

- Does the board receive regular (and meaningful) Compliance updates? Are these of an appropriate quality and detail?

- Am I comfortable with the adequacy of procedures to ensure that the persons involved in the Compliance function are not involved in the performance of services or activities they monitor?

- Am I satisfied that the methods for determining the remuneration of persons involved in the Compliance functions is Remuneration Code compliant and does not compromise objectivity?

- Am I comfortable that the Compliance function is able to (and actually does) operate with the requisite independence?

Compliance monitoring

- Am I satisfied that the level of compliance monitoring activity (including, nature, scope and frequency) is appropriate?

- How often is the sufficiency of compliance monitoring activity reviewed, and by whom? Am I satisfied that this is appropriate?

- Do I understand (and could I articulate) how the Compliance monitoring programme is devised?

Compliance breaches

- Are breaches escalated as appropriate to board/committee level and fully considered? Is explicit consideration given as to whether these breaches are (or may be) indicative of systemic issues? If so, is appropriate action taken?

- Do I challenge and ask searching questions, if necessary – for example, around seemingly implausible explanations or late reports?
- Is there a conscious focus on identifying the underlying root cause(s) of any significant compliance breaches? How does this focus materialise in practice? Is it documented?
- Are 'lessons learned' exercises undertaken where appropriate, as a matter of course?

Comments

The Compliance function is regarded by the Regulator as a crucial independent safeguard for all firms. Accordingly, it will be important to be able to demonstrate, if challenged, that (amongst other things) the Compliance function: is adequately resourced; possesses the requisite expertise and experience; has sufficient stature, visibility and voice internally; operates truly independently, without fear of raising difficult issues; and reports appropriate information to the board and other relevant committees.

The Compliance function is responsible for both advising the business on its adherence with applicable rules and regulations and for monitoring the business's compliance therewith.

In practice, the quality of monitoring activity in particular can be somewhat variable. Unsurprisingly, therefore, the Regulator has taken a keen interest in the overall adequacy of a firm's compliance monitoring programme and related activity – and, indeed, may draw wider adverse inferences (for example, about a firm's risk management framework and general culture) from a perceived deficient approach.

It is vital that any identified compliance breaches are (and are seen to be) taken sufficiently seriously, and escalated to, and overseen at, an appropriately senior level within the governance hierarchy. For example, a significant issue involving substantive potential customer detriment would ordinarily be expected to be escalated up to the board. Conversely, where such an issue is not seen to have been raised to board level, questions may well be asked about the adequacy of a firm's governance arrangements; and, more broadly, about the prevailing internal culture.

As a matter of course, demonstrable consideration should be given to a root cause analysis; and an assessment as to whether the particular issue may be indicative of wider systemic concerns.

It is especially important that searching questions are seen to have been posed, explanations probed and lessons learned.

Disclosure to the Regulator

Questions

- Where relevant, am I sufficiently clear as to my responsibilities to disclose appropriately any information of which the Regulator would reasonably expect notice, and of the importance placed on this responsibility by the Regulator?
- Am I confident that I receive the requisite levels of information to enable me to discharge this responsibility?
- Do I fully appreciate that my responses to regulatory questions must be truthful and not misleading in any respect?

Comments

This responsibility falls upon those individuals within the firm who are responsible for reporting matters to the Regulator. Such person(s) must promptly inform the Regulator of information of which they are aware and which it would be reasonable to assume would be of material significance to the Regulator, whether in response to questions or otherwise.

The Regulator places great store on this particular responsibility as an important source of intelligence and information about firms. Accordingly,[70] a failure to discharge this responsibility may well be regarded as a serious contravention.

Culture

Questions

- Am I sufficiently clear as to the Regulator's cultural expectations?

---

[70] And based on numerous published regulatory sanctions.

- Am I clear as to my role and responsibility in this context?

- Do I appreciate that the Regulator can relatively easily attribute any serious issue(s) or misconduct to a poor culture – in respect of which I may be held ultimately responsible?

- Can I articulate the culture and cultural expectations within my firm?

- Can I provide some illustrative examples of the measures taken to establish and maintain the desired culture?

- Can I provide examples of how the right 'tone from the top' is set and maintained?

- Similarly, can I describe how the right 'tone from the middle' is set and maintained?

- Can I articulate how my firm independently measures/assesses whether the firm (and its staff) are satisfying espoused cultural values and expectations in practice?

- Could I describe some of the key cultural indicators or metrics used in such an assessment?

- Am I confident that staff across the firm are on the same cultural wavelength as the board? How do I gain this assurance?

New Business Opportunities

- Am I comfortable that there is sufficient focus on risk, culture and clients when the firm is contemplating new business opportunities? Is this readily evidenced?

- Is the management information provided sufficiently informative in this respect?

Comments

The Regulator expects the board to articulate and maintain a culture of risk awareness and ethical behaviour.

NEDs must play their part in ensuring that a strong client-centric and compliant culture pervades throughout the organisation. This will include (but not be limited to) ensuring that: (i) the requisite tone from the top is set and reiterated periodically; (ii) culture at all levels of the firm is regularly measured against an agreed set of cultural indicator metrics – to ensure that the day-to-day actions are matching the rhetoric; (iii) any cultural issues (or observed shortfalls against metrics) are appropriately addressed and that lessons are learned, where necessary; (iv) the root causes of any such issues are identified and remedied; and (v) any emerging themes or trends which may be indicative of cultural failings are identified and investigated.

As a reference guide, NEDs might helpfully consult chapter 6.

Illustrative hypothetical scenarios

The Regulator has provided the following illustrative examples of scenarios in which it may consider taking enforcement action against an in-scope NED:

- A Skilled Person Review reveals that a firm's Risk Committee has not advised the Board on the firm's risk appetite nor assisted it in overseeing the implementation of the firm's strategy by executive management in contravention of a specific regulatory requirement. In this situation, the Regulator might primarily consider whether there could be grounds to sanction the Chair of the Risk Committee.

- During a Board Effectiveness Review, the Regulator discovers that the Remuneration Committee has failed to prepare any decisions regarding remuneration for consideration and decision by the Board. In this situation, the Regulator may consider whether there could be grounds to sanction the Chair of the Remuneration Committee.

- A firm's Chairman and in-scope NEDs have serious concerns about an overly dominant CEO. These concerns are not addressed, recorded or discussed by the Board or with the Regulator.

6

C U L T U R E

"There has not been a case of a major prudential or conduct failing in a firm which did not have among its root causes a failure of culture as manifested in governance, remuneration, risk management or tone from the top. Culture has thus laid the ground for bad outcomes, for instance where management are so convinced of their rightness that they hurtle for the cliff without questioning the direction of travel."

Andrew Bailey, CEO of the FCA, 2016

"Culture remains a key driver of significant risks in every sector and the root cause of high-profile and significant failings ... We continue to focus on the culture within firms, and will hold management to account (including through the provisions of the Senior Managers and Certification Regime) where cultural issues lead to internal controls that fail to promote and support the right outcomes for consumers and the market."

"Our focus on culture in financial services firms and its impact on conduct has been, and remains, a priority ... We are interested in the direction of travel of firm's cultures and if indicators show progress."

FCA Business Plan 2016/2017

Backdrop

As the above quotes illustrate, culture is (and will undoubtedly remain) an area of concerted regulatory focus – and not only in the UK (see further below under 'Culture in the US'). For some time now,[71] the Regulator has highlighted the importance of a strong customer-centric and market-oriented culture. This has been characterised variously as a culture of 'should we, not could we'; 'doing the right thing'; 'setting the right example'; and ensuring that the 'right tone from the top' is communicated effectively.

---

[71] Notably, since the LIBOR manipulation scandal.

As implicitly referenced in the last of these quotes – and as expressly confirmed by the Regulator on numerous recent occasions – firms are expected to proactively undertake culture change programmes and to perform periodic culture assessments. Unsurprisingly, the Regulator has not prescribed how such exercises should be conducted – so it remains for firms to formulate an appropriate model, suited to their respective business models, risk profiles and operational set-ups.

"We realise how challenging and complex the topic is for firms and that there is no single right answer across firms. In our supervision of firms, what we're looking for is firms recognising issues and taking robust, consistent and persistent steps to effect change. We want to see that firms are moving in the right direction; with indicators supporting the impression that progress is being made."

Jonathan Davidson, Director of Supervision (12 July 2016)

This chapter offers some thoughts on how cultural assessments might be approached in practice.

Culture through the Regulator's lens

"We define culture as the typical, habitual behaviours and mindsets that characterise a particular organisation. The behaviours are the 'way things get done around her'; they are the way that we act, speak and make decisions without consciously thinking about it."

John Davidson, Director of Supervison, July 2016

How the Regulator measures culture

"We are making our assessment of culture by looking at the examples of behaviours that we come across in supervision and we are looking closely at what management is doing to shape culture and the direction implied in it."

John Davidson, Director of Supervison, July 2016.

The Regulator has outlined four areas, which it considers leaders can use to shape culture:

(i) Tone from the top – how leaders are role modelling the professional culture. Is the culture, or the major determinants of culture, an important and regular item for board discussion? What changes are they making to break with the past?

Middle management are also critically important to the tone from the top and they should not become a permafrost layer.

(ii) Formal, tangible practices and areas which tell people what they need to do to be successful; and ensure that the right people are employed and rise to leadership roles. Clearly, the recruitment, compensation and promotion practices are critical in this regard.

(iii) The narratives that circulate in a firm that explain what the firm is trying to achieve, how it will be achieved and why it is important. Key narratives that the Regulator looks at are the tone of strategies, business plans and mission and value statements. For example, targets: how would, say, asking employees to deliver 10% more year-on-year with 25% less headcount impact on behaviour? If employees feel under pressure to deliver against tough/unrealistic targets, there is a real risk that conduct could slip as a result.

(iv) The organisation's capabilities – leading to a new mindset and set of behaviours. For example, to have a conversation about the needs of customers requires an ability to relate to a customer and problem solve a solution, which is a different competence from the persuasiveness needed to sell a specific product.

Critical areas influencing firm culture

Separately, the Regulator has identified six areas of management behaviour that can influence a firm's culture of customer treatment:

(a) Leadership – all managers should clarify in their practices and communication that the fair treatment of customers is fundamental to the firm's operation.

(b) Strategy – the firm can articulate a clear vision featuring fair treatment of customers. Strategic decisions reflect the centrality of customers to the firm's future. Risk levels should reflect customer concerns and feedback.

(c) Decision-making – at all levels decision-making should reflect on the fair treatment of customers. Feedback from staff, customers and other external sources should be used, where appropriate.

This management information should feed into properly balancing customers' interests against those of shareholders.

(d) Recruitment, training and competence – staff selection and reward should reflect the importance of customer treatment to the firm.

(e) Reward – the firm's reward framework should be transparent and support the fair treatment of customers. In other words, firms should not concentrate on sales, volumes and profit without considering quality and controls to mitigate this risky framework.

(f) Controls – the firm should have integral controls to reflect the fair treatment of customers.

Cultural enforcement

However, the Regulator's focus on culture represents more than just a conceptual area of interest. In a notable development of late, culture has begun to feature increasingly prominently in a number of enforcement cases brought against both firms and senior-level individuals, each essentially underpinned by a finding of significant cultural failings (and[72] brought under the cover of one or more of the relevant Statements of Principle – such as failure to ensure due compliance with the requirements of the regulatory system).

The cases summarised briefly below serve to illustrate a clear direction of travel, leading to a 'new' perceived threat of cultural attribution.

HomeServe (February 2014)

In February 2014, HomeServe received the largest ever retail conduct fine, £30m, for a series of *"serious, systemic and long-running failings"*. While HomeServe operates within the retail sector, the potential 'read-across' onto wholesale businesses is clear.

In broad terms, HomeServe *"failed to embed a robust culture with adequate focus on customers and treating customers fairly"*, Additionally, senior management were found to have been *"insufficiently engaged with compliance matters"*. In particular, HomeServe was criticised for:

• operating a culture of putting profits first;

---

[72] In the case of individuals.

- focusing on quantity, not quality;
- failing to learn lessons from previous incidents;
- failing to accord the Compliance function a meaningful voice and the opportunity to input substantively on relevant issues;
- failing to ensure that the board gave sufficient attention to compliance issues and resolve them – for example, the board failed to review and react to Compliance monitoring reports that raised serious concerns (about the potential mis-selling of products);
- failing to ensure that senior managers received adequate regulatory training – which, in turn, led to an insufficient regulatory awareness to identify issues;
- failing to identify and address inappropriate bias within the remuneration structure for both Sales and Complaints Handling teams; and
- failing to pay due regard to customers' interests.

Swinton (Halpin, Clare and Bowyer) **(November 2014)**

The CEO (Halpin) and two senior Managing Directors (Clare and Bowyer) of Swinton Insurance were fined over £900,000 in aggregate for their roles in Swinton's perceived failure to comply with the requirements of the regulatory system.

In summary, the individuals were criticised for (amongst other things):

- allowing (and even encouraging) a profit-centred culture to develop, at the expense of customers;
- choosing to ignore compliance in favour of profit generation; and
- incentivising senior officers to act in a manner incompatible with customers' interests.

In a stark warning to senior individuals, the FCA commented that:

"Those with significant influence within firms are responsible for setting the tone and culture ... The three former directors did not recognise the risk of this culture developing or take reasonable steps to prevent it."

If it were ever in doubt, the Regulator took this opportunity to reiterate its view that the cultural buck stops with senior management – an assertion with which it is difficult to take serious issue.

Martins (Caplin) (January 2015)

David Caplin was the CEO of RP Martins, an inter-dealer broking firm, which had previously been sanctioned for its role in the LIBOR manipulation scandal. Caplin was pursued separately by the FCA and fined £210,000 – for what the FCA considered to be his failure to:

• ensure effective oversight of compliance, supervision and monitoring of broker conduct; and

• implement externally recommended improvements to compliance.

Significantly, Caplin was found to have *"presided over a firm where the compliance culture was extremely weak"*, and permitted the development of a culture which prioritised profit to the detriment of regulatory compliance.

In a salutary message to senior managers of regulated firms, the FCA commented that:

"This case … should serve as a warning to everyone that holds a SIF that if a firm's misconduct is attributable to cultural failings, then we expect senior management to answer for this."

An obvious concern arising from this statement is the relative ease with which the Regulator is able to attribute misconduct or a significant issue to cultural shortcomings. For instance, it would be easy in principle for the Regulator, applying hindsight judgement, simply to allege that the facts speak for themselves – in other words, to claim the very fact that issues have crystallised/occurred must, by implication, mean that there are serious cultural failings. By playing this 'cultural attribution' card, the Regulator is effectively turning the spotlight directly onto senior management – whom, as seen above, it regards as ultimately responsible for instilling an appropriate culture. Faced with such a challenge, senior managers would effectively be required – the burden of proof having essentially shifted – to demonstrate that they took reasonable steps in the circumstances.

Barclays Bank plc (May 2015)

Barclays was fined over £284 million for its role in the FX market scandal. Over a period of five years, Barclays failed properly to control its London voice trading operations in the FX market, with the result that traders were able to behave in a manner that put Barclays' interests ahead of the interests of clients, other market participants and the wider UK financial system.

Significantly, the FCA observed that *"the right values and culture were not sufficiently embedded in Barclays' FX business"*.

Deutsche Bank AG (April 2015)

Deutsche Bank was fined £226.8 million in relation to its role in the manipulation of IBOR. Notably, cultural failings recur frequently in the Final Notice and essentially underpinned the FCA's case: *"These findings exemplify a culture within Global Markets which either fostered, or failed to search for and root out, systemic deficiencies and conduct risks."*

Sonali Bank (UK) Limited (October 2016)

Sonali Bank was fined £3,250,600 for AML systems and controls failings. The FCA concluded that:

"At the top of the business, despite warnings from board members and from the Internal Auditors, the board and senior management failed to embed a culture of compliance throughout the firm and failed to provide adequate oversight to the MLRO department which was under-resourced. Senior management failed to ensure that SBUK fostered a culture which valued robust adherence to its regulatory responsibilities and allowed a culture of minimal or non-compliance to persist throughout the firm."

Tootell and Alderson (2016)

The *Tootell* and *Alderson* cases, both referenced in chapter 4, provide two further examples of cases in which cultural failings have featured prominently.

Managing cultural enforcement risk

"In our supervision of individual firms what we're looking for is firms recognising issues and taking robust, consistent and persistent steps to effect change."

FCA Director of Supervision, 2016

Pervasive culture

In practice, the Regulator will expect to see demonstrable evidence of a strong compliance culture being driven from the very top of the firm and permeating downwards throughout the organisation.

However, a good 'tone from the top' will not of itself suffice. Instead, and as observed recently by the Regulator, it is essential that the layer of middle management is seen to be setting the right cultural example – as, from experience, it is often at this operational level that cultural issues will materialise.

Indeed, it is also increasingly common for the Regulator to test culture during on-site supervisory visits, by making impromptu requests to speak with junior members of staff, to test whether they are articulating messages consistent with those that the Regulator will likely have heard from senior personnel. Any perceived inconsistencies will be sure to raise questions as to the degree to which culture has been truly institutionally embedded.

Cultural indicators

The Regulator's stance on, and approach to, culture was covered earlier in this chapter. This section addresses the topic from a firm's (practical) viewpoint.

For many, culture is an inherently nebulous concept that is not easily defined. From a practical perspective, culture might most usefully be approached by reference to some commonly observed key cultural indicators.

Response to issues/incidents (including 'near misses'/warning signals)

A firm's response to an incident or issue can often prove to be a key cultural indicator – after all, actions speak louder than words. For example:

- Was the response sufficiently credible? Did it indicate a resolute determination on the firm's part to 'do the right thing'?
  - To whom was it escalated?
  - Who is responsible for dealing with the identified issue?
  - How robustly was it handled?
  - Was it prioritised appropriately, with the requisite sense of urgency?
  - Was there appropriate governance 'around' the response? For example, was a board-mandated steering committee established, where appropriate?
  - Was the Regulator informed in a timely manner?
  - Has an action/remedial plan been instituted?
  - Are deadlines appropriate (that is, seen as sufficiently challenging, but nevertheless realistic)?
  - Was a wider internal investigation appropriate in the circumstances?
  - Were any lessons to be learned? If so, how in practice?

Complaints handling

How seriously is the firm treating complaints? For example:

- Are any trends being monitored effectively and actioned accordingly? By whom?
- Is the complaints-handling process sufficiently transparent and designed to give the complainant a fair hearing? When was this process last reviewed (and by whom)? Is the process in line with prevailing regulatory expectations?
- What complaints-related management information is being generated?
  - To whom is it circulated?

Incentive structures

Is an appropriate balance being struck between the interests of clients and the firm? Is this documented in a formal policy? Is it monitored (and, if so, by whom)?

- To what extent (if at all) is the emphasis on clients' interests/good regulatory compliance conduct, as opposed to revenue generation?
  - Where is this evidenced?
  - What (if any) claw-back mechanisms exist?

Performance management

Are appropriate metrics being used to assess individuals' performance (including as part of bonus, compensation and promotion decisions)? How seriously are contraventions treated in practice?

- Is 'good citizenship' being afforded sufficient weight? Can this be evidenced?
- Is there an over-focus on revenue generation?
- What sanctions are employed for failure to complete mandatory compliance training? Or for material and/or repeated breaches of internal policies and procedures?
  - Are they credible? Is there a true incentive to 'do the right thing'?
- Does the firm have a clear policy outlining the metrics and criteria used in the assessment of performance? Does the firm use a 'balanced scorecard', for example?

Board/senior management engagement

Is the correct 'tone from the top' being conveyed? Does it pervade throughout the organisation?

- How (if at all) have the CEO/senior management articulated their cultural expectations?
  - Where is the evidence? For instance, when did the CEO last issue a relevant communication to all personnel, setting out his or her clear expectations?
  - Is it time for a rearticulation?

- Is the articulation of the firm's cross-selling approach consistent with treating customers fairly (TCF) and with clients' best interests?
- Are they demonstrably practising what they preach?
- To what extent (if at all) will the board/senior management become (and remain) involved in any material regulatory compliance issues? Through what channel(s)?
  - Has there been a recent example? If so, how did it play out?
- What relevant management information (MI) is provided to the board/senior management? Does this, for instance, include any TCF-related information?
- How does the board/senior management ensure that the firm's cultural values are adapted and applied by middle management (i.e., that there is an appropriate 'tone' from the 'middle')?

Management response to audit findings

- Are all action points closed off satisfactorily within an acceptable time-frame?
- Is there appropriate governance and accountability 'around' open action points?

Use of, and response to, employee surveys to help gauge culture

- Does the firm utilise employee surveys in order to gauge cultural attitudes and awareness?
- Questions covering (amongst other things): perceived willingness/ freedom to raise issues; clarity on senior management expectations; approach to errors; sufficiency of training and awareness; consistency of message/conduct across the organisation (for example, are senior staff leading by example?).

Quality of MI

MI will be a key evidential indicator of cultural awareness throughout an organisation, and links into several other areas covered in this chapter.

- Is MI sufficiently informative in the context of customer-facing issues?
- Is MI being provided to the right bodies/individuals within the firm's governance framework?
  - Is MI receiving appropriate challenge? How is this evidenced?
- Is MI prepared to the right level of detail to ensure a proper understanding of issues? Is this periodically reviewed?
- Is MI sufficiently meaningful in its content?

Recruitment/induction process

- Is there sufficient demonstrable focus and emphasis on strong cultural values and compliant behaviour? For instance, are prospective employees presented with 'moral dilemma' scenarios as part of the recruitment process in order to gauge their cultural mindset and attitide?

Approach to training

A firm's approach to training and education can be a good indicator of its attitude towards good compliance conduct.

- What is the firm's general approach to training its personnel?
- What does the training programme look like? Who is responsible for this?
  - Does it appropriately reflect regulatory expectations and evolve over time?
  - Is it sufficiently tailored and practical?
  - Is it undertaken frequently enough?
- Is training mandatory? What checks are in place to ensure that all required participants do in fact attend?
- Are new joiners provided with appropriate induction training?
- Is completion of all required training modules an important factor in appraisals? For example:
  - Are bonuses withheld from any individual who has not successfully completed their training?

Response to legal or regulatory developments

- Is the firm sufficiently responsive to regulatory pronouncements and developments (including relevant published Final Notices)? For example, does the firm routinely undertake 'gap analyses' in response to relevant regulatory pronouncements, such as thematic reports?

- How does the firm monitor for relevant pronouncements and developments (including thematic reports, market studies and speeches)?

- Who is responsible for ensuring that the firm remains in line with prevailing regulatory expectations and developments?

Approach to contraventions of internal requirements

The manner in which breaches of internal requirements are treated will be an important cultural indicator. The Breach Register will often be an obvious first port of call for the Regulator.

- What is the process for investigating policy/procedure breaches?
  - To whom might issues be escalated?
- How are repeated contraventions dealt with?
- What flow-through is there into appraisals/bonus/promotion determinations?
- Is the firm acting in accordance with its stated expectations?
- What does the Breach Register look like? What story does it tell?

Decision-making, challenge and escalation

- Are decisions being taken at the right levels and issues challenged/escalated appropriately?
- Is the rate of challenge/escalation a concern? Are there indications that a 'blame culture' exists, resulting in a reluctance to escalate?
- Are committees appropriately constituted to ensure that culture, conduct and clients' interests are properly represented?
- Is the governance framework readily explicable and justifiable – in particular, from the perspective of cultural oversight/monitoring?

Customer experience
- How customer-friendly was the frontline sales experience?
- How is customer experience monitored, and by whom?

Approach to product development and ongoing product monitoring

Is sufficient weight being attached to TCF and to clients' interests throughout the product development process and beyond into post-sale?

- Do internal templates, processes and New Product Committee minutes adequately reflect customers' interests, or are they solely focused on commercial considerations?
- Are trends actively monitored, and by whom? For example:
  - Are products exceeding all expectations – is there an untoward reason for this?
  - Are products attracting an unusual/inordinate number of complaints or queries?
  - Are products being sold to the type of customers for whom they were originally intended?
  - What post-sale MI is generated? How is this considered, and by whom?

Role/status of Chief Compliance Officer (CCO) and Chief Risk Officer (CRO) within organisational framework

Where do the CCO/CRO feature within the governance framework?

- Do the CCO and CRO have a meaningful voice? Are their views valued in practice?
- What is the extent of their day-to-day contact with senior management?
- What is the internal perception of Compliance/Risk – business prevention versus commercial facilitation?

Relationship with Regulators

Does the firm enjoy a healthy and constructive relationship with the Regulator?

- Does the firm endeavour to remain on the front foot with the Regulator?
- Is the firm sufficiently open and transparent in its dealings with the Regulator?
- Does the CEO meet periodically with the Regulator, with a view to fostering a constructive relationship and rapport?

Measuring culture – periodic audit/assessment

One obvious way in which the risk of cultural attribution can be managed is through a periodic cultural assessment (or audit), conducted by a sufficiently independent function – for instance, Internal Audit or a firm's external auditors. Indeed, as discussed elsewhere in this chapter, such cultural assessments are now essentially a clear regulatory expectation.

The purpose of such a retrospective review would be to assess, honestly and objectively, whether the institution is in fact meeting its stated cultural expectations. In principle, such a review should serve to assist with any defence (should one ever be required) to an allegation that an individual presided over cultural failings to which an incident or misconduct has been attributed by the Regulator. In other words, it should assist in establishing that reasonable steps were taken. Significantly, the output of a cultural assessment of this nature would likely represent the key plank of any defence.

The cultural assessment would measure actual conduct over the previous period against stated cultural expectations (see below for some examples).

It would be advisable for the output of such a review to be documented and reviewed/challenged by senior management and/or the board (as appropriate).

Any material variances from espoused cultural expectations would be analysed to assess whether any lessons are to be learned and/or enhancements required. Results would in turn be reported to senior management or the board.

Outcomes would be incorporated, as appropriate, into compliance monitoring/audit plans and relevant risk assessments.

However, such periodic assessments should not necessarily be regarded solely as a defensive measure – indeed, real value can be derived if these exercises are undertaken properly and with the requisite stakeholder buy-in. In many cases, any changes required will be adjustments to existing practices and/or adopting a modified mind-set or 'lens', rather than radical overhaul. Wheels should not ordinarily need to be reinvented.

It is important to recognise that specific culture pockets may exist within (especially larger) institutions. A firm's approach to measuring culture will need to be tailored accordingly to reflect the differing considerations and risks arising within such areas.

In order to perform a meaningful cultural assessment, an institution will need to carefully articulate its specific cultural expectations in respect of each relevant cultural indicator. This may be done in an overarching values statement, for example:

[Firm] promotes a culture of integrity, openness, accountability and client-centric conduct. Clients' interests [and market integrity] are, and shall remain, at the heart of the way in which we operate. All personnel are expected to behave in a manner that is consistent with these cultural values.

[Firm] has identified a number of specific cultural indicators (together with related expectations), against which [Firm's] conduct will be periodically assessed – to ensure that [Firm] and its employees are, in practice, acting in accordance with stated cultural expectations.

The following examples relate to more specific areas of culture:

(i) Incentive structures/remuneration arrangements
Incentive structures/remuneration arrangements must be transparent and [appropriately] [positively] incentivise and reflect good compliance conduct and client-centric behaviour; and conversely dis-incentivise any form of conduct involving undue risk-taking and any form of non-compliant behaviour.

(ii) Performance management/promotions

The metrics utilised to appraise an individual's performance must [appropriately/meaningfully and demonstrably reflect] [afford due weight to] client-centric, compliant conduct; and not, for example, over-emphasise revenue generation. The outcome of each individual appraisal must be [readily] reconcilable to these expectations.

(iii) Response to issues/incidents

[Firm] will respond credibly and robustly to material issues or incidents. In particular, any such issues/incidents will be expected to have been: escalated appropriately [including to a member of the Executive Committee]; notified to the Regulator in a timely manner (where necessary); duly prioritised, with the requisite sense of urgency; and managed at a suitable level of seniority within an appropriate governance framework [as approved by the board].

Additionally, [Firm] will (where necessary) have formulated an appropriate action/remedial plan, with challenging but realistic deadlines and milestones; and actively consider whether any lessons must be learned; and whether there is any potential 'read-across' to other areas of the business.

(iv) Reporting and handling of employee concerns

[Firm] will actively (and demonstrably) encourage employees to raise any concerns; without fear of any adverse repercussions.

[Firm] will respond appropriately and credibly, by investigating the circumstances behind the concern(s) raised; with a view to ascertaining whether, for example, there may be wider issues which need to be addressed.

[Firm] will deal robustly with any adverse findings arising out of its investigation within an appropriate governance framework.

Measuring culture – other approaches

There is, of course, no single 'right' approach to the measurement of culture. Alternative approaches – which can be used in addition to the periodic assessments discussed above – include:

- Regular staff surveys, focused on issues such as: willingness/ readiness to escalate concerns; perception of the example being set by senior management; and awareness of the firm's cultural values and expectations. Such surveys can also be used to monitor any emerging trends over time – by including the same or similar questions on each occasion.

- An independently run programme of scenario-based workshops, involving a representative cross-section of employees – at varying levels of seniority, in different (front, middle and back office) functions and with different tenures (new joiners and veterans). While certain of the discursive scenarios would be tailored to the particular audience, others would be common across all workshops – to ensure a degree of direct comparability. Each scenario would include one or more relevant 'real life' dilemmas, designed to generate engagement and interaction, and to reveal cultural attitudes and mindset.

By way of example, a scenario might centre around a colleague who is overheard telling fellow colleagues that he enjoyed a *"wonderful day at the races yesterday"* when in fact he had called in sick. Amongst other things, attendees would be asked for their views on the perceived severity of the colleague's actions, how they would likely have responded and how senior management would expect them to have responded.

Observations from the programme, together with any related recommendations, would be documented and considered by senior management/the board.

These approaches to culture are by no means mutually exclusive, and can be regarded as complementary to one another. Any firm wishing to undertake a comprehensive assessment may opt for all of these initiatives at appropriate time intervals.

Culture: the Supervisor's perspective

In a recent report, entitled *Banking Conduct and Culture – A Call for Sustained and Comprehensive Reform*,[73] the influential Group of 30

---

[73] Published July 2015.

proposes a series of questions for supervisors to pose when assessing culture (or a firm's adherence to its values and conduct). These questions, replicated below (and echoing various of the above cultural indicators), may represent a helpful framework against which firms can self-assess. Those points considered to be of particular importance are highlighted in **bold**.

- Are the board and senior management adequately focused on understanding the culture that exists and seeing adherence to firm values and conduct as a strategic imperative for the institution?

- Is this evidenced in practices such as transparency for material transgressions, and owning the responsibility for identifying and dealing with problems?

- Are the firm's values and conduct statements **taken seriously**, and is there consistency among strategy, business model, target returns, risk appetite, incentives, performance assessment, desired conduct and values to support the desired behaviours and outcomes?

- Does the board focus adequately on the embedding of values and conduct by devoting adequate time to these issues, **receiving regular comprehensive reporting on these issues** from a variety of sources, acting on those as necessary and itself participating in the internal communication of the desired behaviours?

- Do the board and committee charters include oversight of values and conduct? How are these matters **reflected** in the work of the board and its committees?

- Do the relevant management bodies and committees have charters that explicitly refer to responsibility for oversight of values, conduct and culture issues, and is sufficient regular management time, energy and focus devoted to these issues?

- Do the CEO and Executive team demonstrate persistent championing throughout the firm of the desired conduct and values?

- **Are the Executive team and mid-level managers engaged**, and are they assessed and compensated on how well they promote and assess conduct and values issues in their teams?

- Do the CEO and Executive team objectives include conduct, values and cultural matters?

- Is an important part of the board's annual evaluation of the CEO and his or her direct reports championing the desired culture and effectively overseeing the embedding of the desired conduct and values and any remediation programme?

- Does the Executive team demonstrate sound understanding of how a chosen remediation programme will achieve results, and does it have ways of measuring progress?

- Does the CEO and Executive team's incentive regime have material financial consequences for managers whose oversight (and living) of desired values and conduct is weak?

- Does the firm celebrate those who live up to the firm's values and desired conduct in difficult circumstances?

- Is there evidence that the firm is using a **balanced scorecard** with input from Compliance, Risk Management and Human Resources, and **with significant weight on *how* results are achieved**?

- Are there robust and comprehensive data to identify alignment with conduct and values by the business, its functional units and individuals?

- Is the Executive team reviewing in detail the top leadership group, and is there use of tools such as 360-degree assessments?

- Are annual appraisals and penalties applied to breaches of cultural norms, values and principles, and not just breaking specific rules of legal requirements?

- When deficiencies are identified, does the firm look at whether similar issues exist in related areas of the firm?

- Is there evidence of **robust internal sanctioning**, with **material consequences** for staff in the event of poor alignment with conduct and values?

- Do the firm's promotion and hiring processes (including for senior management and the CEO) place material weight on compatibility with the desired values and conduct and consistent demonstration of the desired behaviours?

- Is frontline accountability clear?
- Do the frontline management and staff **demonstrate** understanding of, and the ability to identify, values and conduct issues and act accordingly?
- Does frontline management demonstrate the ability to deal with breaches and to assess staff performance?
- Are training and development programmes anchored in cases relevant to the firm, delivered by management and regularly refreshed?
- Is there a clear second line of defence for values and conduct issues with demonstrated input from Human Resources, Compliance and Risk Management?
- Are the second and third lines of defence (that is, Internal Audit) reporting to senior management members to assist their understanding of where the firm stands on conduct and values issues and how any remediation programme is working, and to support governance and oversight responsibilities?
- Do Compliance and Human Resources functions have stature and a proactive preventative mind-set in dealing with these issues?
- Is there a culture of welcoming escalation or self-identification of issues, including the expectation of such conduct, and are there sanctions for wilful blindness?
- Have managers been trained in how to constructively deal with escalation?
- **Is the board satisfied that whistleblowing is treated seriously**, and that staff who raise internal flags are suitably protected and celebrated?

Culture and the SMR

It is apposite to note that two of the Prescribed Responsibilities under the SMR are closely linked to culture:

(i) responsibility for overseeing the adoption of the firm's culture in the day-to-day management of the firm (CEO); and

(ii) responsibility for leading the development of the firm's culture by the governing body as a whole (Chairman).

"While the regulator acknowledges that a firm's culture is a collective matter for the board, these responsibilities seek to ensure that the CEO and Chairman assume a leading role in the development and implementation of the firm's culture."[74]

Accordingly, the Regulator now has an alternative (and likely more convenient) route[75] through which it can pursue perceived culture-related issues or failings.

The guidance in this chapter should represent a helpful framework for both CEOs and Chairmen in this regard.

Culture in the US

As mentioned earlier, culture is not only a major area of focus for the UK Regulator. In the United States, though, culture has featured increasingly prominently in recent regulatory pronouncements. Perhaps unsurprisingly, the underlying themes, expectations and messages are substantively aligned.

By way of a notable example, FINRA, the largest independent regulator for all securities firms conducting business in the US, has identified culture as a distinct area of current focus.[76] FINRA defines culture as *"the set of explicit and implicit norms, practices and expected behaviors that influence how firm executives, supervisors and employees make and implement decisions in the course of conducting a firm's business"*.

In 2016, FINRA committed to formalising its assessment of firm culture, which *"has a profound influence on how a firm conducts its business and manages its conflicts of interest"*. During the appraisals, FINRA will focus on the frameworks that firms use to develop, communicate **and evaluate conformance with** their culture, and will assess five cultural indicators:

*   whether control functions are valued within an organisation (and adequately resourced);

---

[74] Paragraph 2.44, SS28/15.
[75] In addition to any action brought for breach of the Conduct Rules.
[76] FINRA, "2016 Regulatory and Examination Priorities Letter".

- whether policy or control breaches are tolerated;
- whether the organisation proactively seeks to identify risk and compliance events;
- whether supervisors are effective role models of firm culture; and
- whether sub-cultures that may not conform to overall corporate culture are identified and addressed.

More specifically, FINRA will be reviewing how firms establish, communicate and implement cultural values, and whether cultural values are guiding business conduct.

"As part of this review, we plan to meet with executive business, compliance, legal and risk management staff ... to discuss cultural values. We would also like to discuss how your firm communicates and reinforces those values directly, implicitly and through its reward system. **We are particularly interested in how your firm measures compliance with its cultural values, what metrics, if any, are used and how you monitor for implementation and consistent application of those values throughout your organisation."**[77]

The emphasis on ongoing measurement of culture is noteworthy.

FINRA's pre-assessment information request list[78] is also instructive as it indicates particular areas of focus from which conclusions will ultimately be drawn:

1. A summary of the key policies and processes by which the firm establishes cultural values (including whether this is a board-level function at the broker-dealer or at the corporate parent of the firm). A description of any steps initiated or completed in the past two years to promote, strengthen or change the firm's culture.

2. A description of processes employed by executive management, business unit leaders and control functions in establishing, communicating and implementing the firm's cultural values. Include a description of how executive management communicates, promotes and establishes a 'tone from the top' as it relates to

---

[77] FINRA, "Establishing, Communicating and Implementing Cultural Values", February 2016, sent to all relevant firms ahead of the FINRA culture assessment visit.
[78] Sent to all relevant firms ahead of the FINRA culture assessment visit.

cultural values. Also include a description of the firm's approach to ensure that its cultural values are adopted and applied by middle management.

3. A description of how the firm assesses and measures the impact of cultural values (to the extent that assessments and measures exist) and whether they have made a difference in achieving the desired behaviours. Provide a summary of the policy statements, procedures, mission statements or other related documents that reflect the firm's assessments and measures.

4. A summary of the processes the firm uses to identify policy breaches, including the types of reports or other documents the firm relies on, in determining whether a breach of its cultural values has occurred.

5. A description of how the firm addresses cultural value policy or process breaches once discovered. What efforts are used to promptly address these breaches? What is the escalation process to raise and resolve such breaches?

6. A description of the firm's policies and processes, if any, to identify and address sub cultures within the firm that may depart from or undermine the cultural values articulated by the board and senior management.

7. A description of the firm's compensation practices and how they reinforce the firm's cultural values.

8. A description of the cultural value criteria used to determine promotions, compensation or other rewards. Describe opportunities for promotion to the managing director or equivalent level available to personnel of the compliance, legal, risk and audit functions.

All firms – whether or not US-regulated – might usefully employ this checklist as a practical self-assessment tool against which they can benchmark current practices to identify potential areas of weakness I scope for improvement.

7

ATTESTATIONS

Backdrop

I n the wake of the banking crisis and the recent LIBOR and FX scandals, the Regulator has been heavily criticised for its perceived failure to hold several high-profile senior banking executives to account.

The relatively small number of successful enforcement actions brought to date against members of senior management is widely attributed to evidential difficulties in establishing the requisite personal culpability.[79] For instance, in many cases, a CEO (or other senior office holder) will have been several organisational levels removed from the scene of any regulatory failing – presenting an often insurmountable evidential hurdle for the Regulator.

In something of a pragmatic response, the Regulator has adopted a (now familiar) practice of requesting formal attestations from senior individuals within regulated institutions.

An attestation – now a formal supervisory tool – is a personal commitment (provided to the Regulator) from a designated senior approved person that specific action has been or will be taken; or that their firm is compliant in certain stated respects. The Regulator will sometimes prescribe the precise form of wording to be included within the attestation.[80] Attestation requests may be addressed to all firms in an industry sector; alternatively, they may be firm specific – for example, resulting from a recent supervisory visit.

"Our aim is to ensure that there is clear accountability and senior manager focus on those specific issues where we would like to see change within firms.

---

[79] See chapter 3.
[80] As was the case in 2012, with letters sent to the CEOs of larger institutional asset managers in relation to Conflicts of Interest compliance.

We usually ask for attestations to be given by the most relevant significant influence function holder (for example, the SIF who is responsible for the area of the firm at which the issue has arisen or which is responsible for addressing the issue)."[81]

This chapter explores the regulatory risks faced by those individuals required to provide such attestations to the Regulator, and suggests some practical mitigants.

Attestation scenarios

The Regulator has confirmed that the most typical scenarios in which attestations will be used are:

Notification

For emerging risks at firms which are unlikely to result in material consumer detriment or negative impact on market integrity, the Regulator may ask an appropriate individual at a firm to attest that they will notify the Regulator if the risk changes in its nature, magnitude or extent. The responsibility of the attestor is to ensure that the firm appropriately monitors the risk and makes any appropriate notifications.

Undertaking

Where the Regulator requires a firm to take specific action within a particular timescale but the risk is one which is unlikely to result in material consumer detriment or have a negative impact on market integrity, the Regulator may ask for an attestation undertaking that the action will be taken.

Self-certification

For more significant issues, but where the Regulator is confident that a firm can resolve the issue itself, the Regulator may ask for an attestation that the risks have been mitigated or resolved.

---

[81] In the FCA's own words – as per a letter sent to a number of financial institutions.

Verification

In cases in which the Regulator not only mandates a firm to resolve issues or mitigate risks but also requires verification, the Regulator may ask for an attestation confirming that the action, including verification as appropriate (for example, by Internal Audit), has been satisfactorily undertaken.

The underlying legal basis of attestation requests

A frequently raised question is the legal basis upon which the Regulator is entitled to make attestation requests. Whilst an in-depth legal analysis is beyond the scope of this publication, the Regulator's stance is outlined below[82]:

"Principle 11 (Relations with Regulators) of the Principles of Business and Principle 4 of the Statements of Principle for Approved Persons require firms and approved persons to deal with the Required Action described in this letter in an open and co-operative way. The FCA may treat a failure to comply with the Required Action described in this letter as a breach of the Principles (referred to above) and action may be taken as required and appropriate. The firm may be in breach of other (underlying) provisions in the FCA Handbook, e.g. SUP 15 (Notification requirements)."

On this basis, a refusal to provide an attestation may well be regarded as a failure to cooperate. Therefore, for the vast majority, refusal is not a realistic option.

Regulatory exposure

In practice, it is likely that attestors will be Senior Managers. As such, they will be subject to the (Senior Manager) Conduct Rules discussed earlier. As we have seen, a general theme underpinning these responsibilities is a requirement to exercise a reasonable standard of conduct. In the context of attestations, this is likely to translate into a need to:

* ensure that one is adequately informed of relevant matters, and make enquiries of all relevant stakeholders;

---

[82] See previous footnote.

- duly consider and challenge information presented and assurances provided;
- take due care before delegating and not over-delegate;
- arrive at reasonable (and readily justifiable) conclusions; and
- challenge implausible or unsatisfactory explanations.

An attestation-related individual enforcement action might, for example, be brought under the cover of an alleged failure to act with the requisite due skill, care and diligence, and/or to ensure due compliance with the requirements and standards of the regulatory system.

For completeness, an attestor is also potentially vulnerable to the criminal offence of knowingly or recklessly giving the Regulator information which is materially false or misleading – albeit that this imposes a greater burden of proof on, and a higher threshold test for, the Regulator.[83]

Mitigating the risk – practicalities

In order to mitigate the perceived enforcement risks associated with provision of an attestation, an attestor would be well advised to ensure that:

- any delegated work underlying the attestation is entrusted to appropriate functions or personnel – such as Compliance, Risk or certain relevant business line heads;
- all necessary areas touched by the attestation have been covered satisfactorily;
- assurances are requisitioned from all relevant parts of the business/organisation;
- external advice is sought (and attendant comfort received), where appropriate;
- all assurances/comfort received are carefully considered and subjected to a demonstrable challenge process by the attestor;

---

[83] Punishable by fine under section 398 FSMA.

an increasingly common practice is for a chain of back-to-back attestations provided by relevant functions up to the attestor;

- if the attestation is being provided on behalf of the board, it has been duly pre-approved by the directors; and

- there is a clearly documented audit trail of the underlying measures taken by the attestor prior to provision of the attestation – demonstrating that all necessary thought and care was applied.

In this way, an attestor should be well placed to demonstrate (if ever challenged) that he or she took all reasonable measures; in other words, that he or she could not reasonably have been expected to do more in the circumstances prior to the provision of the attestation.

Framing and contextualisation

As a general rule, it will be important for the attestation itself to be properly framed and contextualised – especially in scenarios involving a prescribed form of wording. In practice, this can have the benefit of overlaying helpful additional contextual considerations without necessarily having to modify the prescribed wording itself. In turn, this may serve to positively influence any subsequent scrutiny of the attestation by the Regulator.

Prescribed-form attestations: to qualify or not to qualify?

As mentioned, some attestation requests will prescribe a form of wording. In such cases, the question often arises as to whether it would be acceptable or sensible to qualify this wording in some respect(s).

There is no single right answer to this question. However, it may be prudent to pre-agree with the Regulator any proposed material amendments. Clearly, it would be important to be able to explain, credibly, why the suggested modifications are necessary. Whilst there can be no guarantee of a receptive response, such an approach has on occasion led to a more acceptable compromise formulation.

When attestations were first introduced, there was some concern that **any** qualifications to the prescribed-form wording may be regarded as a red flag by the Regulator and prompt close scrutiny. However, this concern seems to have been assuaged to some degree over time –

with firms seemingly less nervous about broaching with the Regulator the proposed qualification of the attestation.

Limiting scope and clarification

Notwithstanding the Regulator's assertion that attestations *"need to be specific, achievable and have demanding but realistic timelines"*,[84] in certain cases there will still be a need to clarify and, where appropriate, limit the terms of the attestation requirements. While there can of course be no guarantees that the Regulator would accede to any such requests, these issues are nevertheless worth raising at the outset. Again, it will be important to explain cogently why the request is being made, and the likely adverse consequences if no changes are permitted.

It is not unknown for the Regulator to agree to clarify and/or limit the provisions of an attestation request following such an approach. As typically with any other regulatory dialogue in this context, this should be viewed and conducted as a constructive, rather than adversarial, process.

Wrong nominated attestor?

In some cases, a question may arise over the appropriateness of the Regulator's choice of designated attestor. For example, another senior-level individual might be a more obvious (and suitable) candidate, given the subject matter and coverage of the attestation. Again, in such cases, this should be discussed at the outset with the Regulator, and a cogent explanation provided as to the reasons behind any suggested change.

Post-attestation monitoring

It should be assumed that the Regulator will expect to be notified of any subsequent event that impacts materially on the accuracy of any previously provided attestation. Failure to do so could well expose a

---

[84] Letter from Clive Adamson (then Director of Supervision, FCA) to Graham Beale (Chairman, FCA Practitioner Panel), 22 August 2014.

firm or relevant individual to an allegation of a failure to act openly and cooperatively.

It follows that firms should remain conscious of the terms of all attestations provided to ensure that there has been no intervening event which renders a prior attestation materially incorrect or misleading – in other words, that at least necessitates an update to the Regulator.

Practically, firms should therefore consider whether an attestation is of a nature that its subject matter and the confirmations therein are prone to becoming out of date and would require a subsequent update – for example, because it may refer to a certain state of affairs existing at the time. Any attestations falling into this category should be revisited periodically to ensure that they remain materially true and accurate, and are not misleading. Such a periodic review process might, for example, be incorporated into the firm's business-as-usual assurance framework.

Conclusion

Attestation requests have emerged as a key feature of the Regulator's toolkit, and arguably represent the single greatest form of direct personal regulatory exposure for attesting Senior Managers. Attestors should be under no illusions that their confirmations bring with them a heightened risk of a personal enforcement action – in the event that the attestation is subsequently discovered to have been unfounded.

Accordingly, it will take a brave attestor to 'sign on the dotted line', without first having taken measures along the lines suggested to mitigate this risk down to an acceptable level.

8

THE DIRECTORS' DILEMMA

Introduction

The heightened regulatory focus on senior individual accountability has prompted a number of regulated firm boards to reassess the duality of their respective legal and regulatory responsibilities. This chapter explores how the apparent divergence between legislative requirements and prevailing regulatory expectations in this context might be addressed in practice.

Legal context

In the UK, a company director owes a set of statutory duties to his or her company. One of these legal duties is to act in a way that the director considers, in good faith, would be most likely to promote the success of the company for the benefit of its members as a whole. In doing so, a director must have regard (amongst other matters) to certain additional considerations and stakeholder interests – including community/environmental impact, employee interests and business relationships with suppliers and customers. It appears to be generally accepted that a director's primary and overriding duty is therefore to act in the interests of shareholders.[85] Further, it is only the shareholders who would be entitled to sue in this context.[86]

Regulatory backdrop

A director of an authorised firm must additionally discharge certain regulatory responsibilities – essentially underpinned by a general concern to ensure that the interests of that firm's clients (or customers)[87] remain appropriately safeguarded at all times. Directors of listed companies – whether authorised or not – will also have

---

[85] Or, possibly, creditors, for companies in a financial predicament.
[86] Assuming that the company itself opts not to sue.
[87] And, to a degree, market integrity.

specific market-related considerations to factor into their decision-making processes.[88]

Moreover, and in furtherance of the FCA's consumer protection objective, regulatory pronouncements now invariably refer to the need for firms to put the interests of their customers at the heart of how they run their business, and to ensure that clients' interests are (and remain) central to business models and strategies. Accordingly, from the Regulator's perspective at least, it is abundantly clear that customers' interests are paramount – and should not be subordinated to those of any other stakeholder group (including shareholders).

With a discernible increase in FCA/PRA requests to attend board meetings and/or to review board (or committee) minutes, it is also evident that the Regulator expects to observe – as a reality – the due and demonstrable consideration of clients' interests across boardroom tables.

Relative risk assessment

The results of a recent straw poll suggest that directors of regulated firms believe that the likelihood of a regulatory investigation for failure to discharge their regulatory responsibilities is – in practice – materially greater than that of an action being brought for breach of their statutory duties. Additionally, the directors surveyed considered that the probability of a sanction ultimately being levied (post-investigation) was significantly higher under the regulatory regime. Notably, such sentiments were said to have been influenced by (amongst other things) the recently observed increase in regulatory demands for formal attestations[89] and the onset of the SMR – a significant and concerning development for many.

Nevertheless, these directors clearly understood that they had to comply with both sets of responsibilities.

---

[88] Specific consideration of the Listing Rule and Disclosure & Transparency Rule regimes is beyond the scope of this publication.
[89] See chapter 7.

Dichotomy of interests

The interests of clients and those of shareholders will not always be aligned – indeed, they may often appear to be polarised.

A simple example serves to illustrate this dichotomy: a regulated firm (Firm X) is concerned that its level of profitability has been dipping over recent years in light of harsh market conditions. Shareholders are losing patience and agitating for action. The firm's only realistic chance of remaining in profit is to implement a drastic cost-reduction programme. As a necessary component of this programme, certain control functions will have to be significantly scaled back – including Compliance, Risk and Internal Audit.

The directors of Firm X are of course keen to discharge their legal and regulatory responsibilities. However, in such a scenario, these may be viewed as seemingly irreconcilable – particularly given the inevitable reduction in capacity and consequent effectiveness of the independent control functions – with their customer-focused oversight roles. How, therefore, should the directors respond?

Striking the right balance

A decision to proceed with the proposed cost-reduction programme as planned could clearly be seen as serving shareholders' interests – with increased profitability as the principal driver. Conversely, a wholesale refusal to implement the programme could be regarded as beneficial to the interests of Firm X's customers – on the basis that the programme may have a potentially detrimental impact upon customers – by virtue of materially reduced control function capacity, effectiveness and oversight.

However, each of these approaches could be viewed as effectively excluding the interests of customers and shareholders, respectively – a potentially difficult stance to justify, if subsequently challenged.

The directors of Firm X may therefore decide that the only viable (and appropriate) course is to execute the programme, but only to the extent that customers' interests will, with a reasonable degree of assurance, remain appropriately safeguarded (the Preferred Solution). Such an approach carries the obvious merit of paying demonstrable regard to both customer and shareholder interests.

From the customers' perspective: under the Preferred Solution, the directors of Firm X might be well advised to obtain satisfactory assurances from all relevant internal stakeholders that the planned cost-cutting measures will not, in fact, be likely to prejudice the interests of customers. In practice, this may involve requisitioning internal reports intended to explain, cogently and persuasively, how the interests of customers will remain appropriately protected in light of the proposed cutbacks. For example, the directors might wish to understand (amongst other things) how the Compliance, Risk and Internal Audit functions will continue to be able to ensure that customers' interests will remain satisfactorily safeguarded, notwithstanding the measures envisaged. Accordingly, the member(s) of senior management responsible for these functions might be tasked with preparing a paper for board consideration and to attend the board meeting at which the paper was tabled – to take questions and respond to challenges.

The concerns or issues raised, actions commissioned and challenges made by the directors would be clearly minuted, as would the form(s) of assurance received. Ideally, the documented board considerations should, on their face, leave no obvious questions unanswered or doubts unresolved.

From the shareholders' perspective: the interests of shareholders are also taken into account under the Preferred Solution – albeit in conjunction with the interests of customers. It will be important here for the directors to be able to demonstrate that the ultimate solution chosen was underpinned by a consideration of shareholders' interests – at least insofar as can reasonably be expected in the particular circumstances. In the current regulatory climate, it would take a brave board to sanction a course of action that it considers will be likely to adversely impact customers' interests – irrespective of the fact that such a decision may have been driven by an honest and well-meaning desire to discharge legal duties to shareholders.

Faced with such a dilemma, the directors of Firm X will need to strike an appropriate balance between: (i) pushing the cost-reduction programme as far as possible for the benefit of shareholders; and (ii) ensuring, with a reasonable degree of confidence, that customers' interests will remain properly safeguarded. In other words, the planned cost-reduction exercise can proceed to the extent that customers' interests remain duly protected.

Few would dispute that the potential repercussions of a regulatory investigation[90] and any subsequent related sanction would likely result in financial and/or reputational damage to the firm, thereby diminishing shareholder value and making the Preferred Solution somewhat easier to justify from a legal duties perspective. Indeed, such an interconnection will often in practice prove helpful in enabling boards to reconcile their respective responsibilities and explain the approach taken.

Interestingly, the potentially divergent interests of customers and shareholders, and the attendant need for a balance to be struck, have been expressly acknowledged by the Regulator. The Chief Executive of the FCA has recently observed that firms must strike a balance between profitability and treating customers fairly, whilst at the same time acknowledging "the difficulty for firms of balancing prudential soundness and profitability, with good consumer outcomes".

Practicalities

Directors of regulated firms will almost inevitably encounter such legal/regulatory predicaments from time to time. Whilst every case will, of course, need to be considered on its own facts, the following practical pointers might usefully be borne in mind in relevant scenarios:

Striking the right balance – directors should appreciate and understand that an appropriate balance will often need to be struck in practice. The exclusive consideration of one stakeholder group's

---

[90] It should be noted that the FCA now has the power to publicise enforcement action much earlier in the investigatory process – long before the firm has had the opportunity to make representations and the eventual outcome has been determined.

interests (be it those of shareholders or customers) may prove difficult to justify.

Demonstrability is key – the importance of well-reasoned written evidence cannot be overstated. In practice, it will be vital for directors to be able to point to documentary evidence (for example, board minutes) demonstrating:

- that the board acknowledges its legal and regulatory responsibilities;
- that both customers' and shareholders' interests were in fact taken into account;
- how they were taken into account; and
- how the ultimate decision was reached – including, for example:
  - key underlying considerations;
  - any qualifications/restrictions/conditions imposed by the board in sanctioning a particular course of action – for example, to ensure that the interests of customers will remain sufficiently well protected; this may include a post-implementation review;
  - any forms of assurance received by the board – intended to help evidence the measures taken by the board to satisfy itself that all necessary interests are being appropriately considered and safeguarded; and
  - any challenges made by the board and how these were determined.

If in doubt, advice should be sought[91] – in the current regulatory environment, regulatory interest is high and corresponding tolerance thresholds low.

Conclusion

Directors of regulated firms will occasionally find themselves between the perceived 'rock' of regulatory responsibilities and the 'hard place'

---

[91] Indeed, a broad analogy might be drawn with scenarios in which boards of companies in financial difficulty will often seek advice on the question of whether they should be acting in shareholders' or creditors' interests.

of statutory duties. The solution will often involve a delicate balancing of shareholder and customer interests.

In the current regulatory environment, it might prudently be assumed that the Regulator will take a keen interest in such scenarios. As suggested, a cogent documented audit trail will be essential. Indeed, it is difficult to conceive how a board might otherwise, in practice, convince an inquisitive Regulator, applying hindsight judgement, that its expectations have been met and the firm's responsibilities discharged.

9

PRACTICALITIES

This chapter is relevant to all Senior Managers, regardless of their specific role and responsibilities. Its purpose is to highlight a range of additional practical considerations, not expressly covered elsewhere in this publication. Topics include:

- the importance of demonstrability;
- adopting the right mindset;
- handling regulatory interviews; and
- setting the right 'tone from the top'.

A number of 'real-life' scenarios have also been included – intended to illustrate and draw together some of the key themes and messages for Senior Managers.

The importance of demonstrability

Senior Managers will stand the best chance of refuting any regulatory challenge if they are able to point to hard (that is, documentary) evidence underpinning the reasonableness of their conduct (which, as discussed earlier, is likely to represent the basis of any defence). Indeed, recent experience suggests that senior individuals who are unable to corroborate their defence with any such evidence are unlikely to be able to satisfy the Regulator of the reasonableness of their conduct. In other words, the Regulator may well doubt that an event really happened if there is no supporting documentary evidence. An unfair working presumption perhaps, but reality nonetheless.

Translated into practice, this will mean the Senior Manager being able to demonstrate that, for example:

- relevant/material issues were given due (and balanced) consideration/challenge;
- all feasible options/alternatives were duly considered;

- advice was sought, where appropriate – whether internally from, say, Legal or Compliance, or externally, from counsel; and

- assurances were received, as appropriate, from relevant stakeholders and functions.

Where possible, relevant matters would be evidenced through meeting minutes, file notes and other forms of contemporaneous documentary correspondence/records (such as email follow-ups). While this does not, of course, mean that every last piece of dialogue, deliberation and thought process must be studiously recorded, it nevertheless requires an ongoing awareness of those matters or issues most likely (or with the greatest potential) to attract subsequent regulatory scrutiny. As an informal rule of thumb, a Senior Manager might usefully consider whether the matter at hand has real potential to 'come back to bite them'. In many cases, this will be reasonably self-evident – one way or the other.

Furthermore, Senior Managers should, where possible, ensure that all such documentation is stored in an accessible and readily identifiable manner – not least because the Regulator has a six-year[92] window within which it can pursue a Senior Manager in this context. Indeed, this guidance may prove to be of particular significance for a Senior Manager who is no longer in the employ of the firm but is facing regulatory scrutiny relating to issues arising during his or her tenure at the firm, where the documentation concerned is stored on the firm's systems.

Additionally, Senior Managers might usefully consider whether they should maintain their own personal log of key information and documents.

Post-SMR changes in practice

Arguably, the single most significant shift in practice observed since the SMR came into force is the greater discipline and rigour with which Senior Managers are recording material discussions or decisions outside of board or committee meetings. Most notably, this can be witnessed in the context of oversight of direct reports and delegates.

---

[92] And possibly greater – see chapter 3.

Of course, some may contend that this is little more than good practice in any event.

Adopting the right mindset

From a risk-mitigation perspective, Senior Managers would ideally approach their roles with:

- a concerted and discernible focus on clients' best interests, never allowing these to be (or even to be perceived as being) effectively subordinated to the firm's own commercial interests or those of its shareholders;

- a conscious and consistent regard to the following questions: How would this look to the Regulator? How comfortable would I feel if I had to justify this course of conduct? Have I cut any obvious corners?;

- an appreciation that, as time passes and developments occur, periodic 'take stock' reviews will inevitably be required – for example, systems and controls will need to evolve as risks change. While this undoubtedly requires a degree of discipline, it has become an effective prerequisite for Senior Managers. In short, there is no room for complacency;

- an awareness that the Regulator expects Senior Managers to be focused on (and speak in terms of) risks and attendant controls;

- a desire to ensure that they are kept abreast of, and understand, prevailing regulatory expectations, and in particular appreciate 'where the Regulator is coming from' on topical issues of the day (for example, culture and conduct risk); and

- a healthy scepticism – for example, raising challenges and posing searching questions, where appropriate, and not just blindly relying.

While, for many, this may require an adjustment to a mindset that feels somewhat unnatural, prudent Senior Managers wishing to manage their own personal regulatory exposure would be well advised to think in these terms.

Handling regulatory interviews

In the current regulatory environment, the likelihood of a Senior Manager having, at some point, to attend an interview with the Regulator is high – whether as part of the initial approval process, during a supervisory or thematic visit, or, possibly, within the context of an enforcement action.

What to expect

Whatever the context of the interview, it is likely that there will be multiple interviewers, sometimes representing different areas from within the Regulator's organisation – for instance, Authorisations, Supervision or Enforcement.

It would be prudent to assume that the session will be challenging; anything less can be regarded as a bonus.

Preparation

Interviewees should also be prepared for differing levels of industry and firm-specific knowledge to be displayed from within the interviewing team. For instance, it may be necessary to explain at a relatively fundamental level what type of business is undertaken, how and by whom, how the firm/business is structured and how it operates in practice.

Interviewees should ensure that they have read and digested any internal document packs supplied to assist them with their preparations. It would also be helpful for interviewees to be readily able to discuss: the remit of any committees on which they sit; the risk management and governance frameworks; how any pre-existing significant issues are being handled; and any particularly pertinent recent regulatory developments.

Key messages to be conveyed

Ordinarily, it will be important for certain key messages to be conveyed during any regulatory interview, for example:

- I understand my role and can articulate my attendant regulatory responsibilities;
- I take my regulatory responsibilities very seriously;
- I understand (and can describe at a high level) the firm's risk management and governance frameworks;
- I have a strong awareness of the key inherent risks posed by my business, and the related controls employed to manage those risks;
- I understand (and can articulate) the key conduct risks faced by my firm and business area, and the attendent mitigating controls;
- I appreciate the importance of a strong regulatory compliance culture, driven from the top;
- wherever possible, I can back up my responses with recent practical illustrations – actions speak louder than words;
- I (and the firm) have a concerted client-centric focus, with clients' interests at the heart of our business model and strategy;
- I am aware of the key potential conflicts of interest arising within my area of responsibility and can explain how these are managed in practice;
- I have a good grasp of relevant regulatory hot spots and areas of current concern; and
- I challenge regularly and do not blindly rely.

Dos and don'ts during regulatory interviews

Do:

- be prepared and consider offering up a summary of your role/ function (and where you fit into the grander scheme) at the outset of the meeting; a few presentational slides should suffice;
- convey an overall impression of openness and willingness to cooperate;
- provide clear, factual responses to the questions;
- contextualise responses, where appropriate;
- provide practical illustrations to support responses;
- ask for clarification, if unsure; and

- correct any apparent interviewer misapprehensions.

Don't:

- appear defensive or evasive – which may arouse a degree of suspicion;
- attempt to hijack the meeting;
- feel obliged to fill in awkward pauses/silences;
- go 'off-piste';
- leave the interviewer(s) labouring under any misapprehensions;
- be disingenuous;
- allow any personal bugbears to contaminate your responses (or their tone);
- become argumentative or irritated, or get drawn into protracted debates; and
- bluff a response if you do not know the answer; instead, refer the interviewer(s) to the person best placed to answer.

Setting the right 'tone from the top'

As discussed in chapter 6, 'Culture', Senior Managers are expected to lead – and be seen to lead – by example. In this context, actions really do speak louder than words. In practice, this is likely to involve demonstrable conduct through which the Senior Manager can be seen to be setting the right 'tone from the top' – for example:

- periodic communiqués to staff, reinforcing the importance of regulatory compliance and the low tolerance threshold for any contraventions;
- robust treatment of any significant issues (including matters of a disciplinary nature); and
- the imposition of meaningful sanctions in response to any compliance/procedure-related issues (such as non-completion of mandatory training and repeated personal account dealing breaches); for instance, withholding or denying bonus payments and/or promotions.

Scenarios

The following scenarios are intended to 'bring to life' various of the key themes and messages considered earlier. Unless indicated otherwise, the scenarios apply to Senior Managers holding both executive and non-executive roles.

Scenario 1

Your directors' pack for a forthcoming board/Exco meeting includes a report – for urgent consideration – entitled 'Proposal to expand into high cost short term lending – opportunistic acquisition'. The report has been prepared by the head of the bank's retail lending business.

On reading the report, you observe that there is a seemingly compelling commercial rationale, and a significant (albeit time-critical) opportunity to be seized. The proposition is also positioned as being directly aligned with the CEO's clear desire to innovate and find new sustainable revenue streams.

However, you cannot help but feel that the report presents a rather one-sided assessment of the proposition, with little discernible reference to risk and the potential down-side(s).

How do you react?

Commentary

It is important that you understand the risks of expanding the business into new areas. A failure to do so may well be considered a breach of your obligation to act with due, skill care and diligence, and could, potentially, preclude you from demonstrating 'reasonable steps' if you are alleged to have breached the duty of responsibility

Accordingly, at the board/Exco meeting, you might usefully have queried (amongst other things):

* why the report paid such little apparent regard to risk-related considerations (for example, was this attributable to a governance shortcoming?);
* what risks had been identified in relation to the proposition (and by whom);

- the relative significance of the identified risks;
- what assurances and controls would be in place to mitigate against those identified risks; and
- whether/how the proposition was considered to be consistent with the bank's stated risk appetite.

Any outstanding questions should be answered and any follow-up actions undertaken – to your (and the board/Exco's) satisfaction.

It will, of course, be important that these issues are appropriately reflected in the relevant minutes.

Scenario 2

You have noticed that the last three quarterly Compliance reports have referenced (different) transaction reporting breaches (all of which had been duly notified to the Regulator). On each occasion, the issue was described as being of an 'isolated' nature.

You are concerned that a worrying pattern is emerging that may be indicative of wider systemic transaction reporting issues and, in particular, doubts over adequacy of the relevant systems and controls.

What do you do?

Commentary

In this scenario, you would be expected to raise your concern and seek (sufficiently independent) assurances that the relevant systems and controls really are adequate and fit for purpose. For instance, this may involve the commissioning of an independent review, undertaken by Internal Audit or an external specialist, culminating in a report with observations, conclusions and recommendations.

It would be important for any resulting recommendations to be duly considered and implemented in a timely manner (unless there are justifiable reasons not to do so).

Failure to respond in such a way may expose you to an allegation that you failed to take reasonable steps to ensure that the business for which you are responsible complies with relevant regulatory requirements.

The Regulator specifically highlights the following expectations in this context (amongst various others):

- you should take reasonable steps to inform yourself adequately about the reason why significant breaches (suspected or actual) may have arisen;

- you should take reasonable steps to ensure that identified issues are dealt with in a timely manner. You may need to obtain expert opinion on the adequacy and efficacy of the systems and procedures; and

- you should take reasonable steps to ensure that systems of control are reviewed and, if appropriate, improved, following identification of significant breaches.

You may also be adjudged as having failed to act with the requisite skill, care and diligence.

Scenario 3 (following directly on from Scenario 2)

You voice your concerns at the next board/Exco meeting. The board/ Exco resolves to delegate the investigation into this perceived issue to the Head of Compliance for the area of the business in which these issues have arisen. The Head of Compliance is asked to report back to the board/Exco within six weeks, with observations and recommendations.

Two months pass, with no sign of the report from the Head of Compliance. After a further month, a draft report is circulated by the Head of Compliance to the directors, for consideration at the next board/Exco meeting.

The draft report contains a number of seemingly unsubstantiated assurances and conclusions, and, generally, reads as though it has been compiled in haste, glossing over several important considerations.

Commentary

In the first instance, it is questionable whether the investigation was appropriately delegated to the Head of Compliance for the relevant business area. It is possible that the Compliance function could, to some degree at least, be held responsible for the occurrence of these issues – for example, if shortcomings in compliance monitoring activity had allowed the pattern of issues to materialise. Accordingly, it would have been preferable for the investigation to have been delegated to a party with no potential (or perceived) vested interest – for example, an external law firm. As a general matter, you may well be expected to challenge the independence/suitability of a proposed appointee.

The draft report was not delivered on schedule. This may have caused you to question whether there were any untoward reasons for the delay, and to seek satisfactory assurances that the report will shortly be available. If such assurances were not forthcoming, then it may have been appropriate for a suitable replacement to be appointed.

The draft report contains numerous unsubstantiated conclusions and assurances. You should not accept these, without more. If the basis upon which assurances have been provided and conclusions reached is not evident, then you should request such further detail and elaboration as to satisfy yourself that the conclusions and assurances are robust and underpinned by sound reasoning. Any residual doubts should be aired and, as appropriate, resolved.

Regulatory guidance provides (amongst other things) that the failure to take personal action where progress is unreasonably slow, or where implausible or unsatisfactory explanations are provided, is behaviour that will contravene your obligation to 'take reasonable steps to ensure that any delegation of your responsibilities is to an appropriate person and that you oversee the discharge of the delegated responsibility effectively'.

Scenario 4

The latest board/Exco pack includes detailed financial information for various business areas (alongside, for comparison, the previous year's equivalent figures). You see that the revenues of one business have increased over the past year by ~300%. The associated footnote indicates that this increase is attributable to a newly launched product.

How do you respond?

Commentary

While the ~300% revenue increase could be entirely legitimate, you would nevertheless be expected to have raised a query – to satisfy yourself that there were no untoward factors at play.

A failure to question this exceptional revenue increase may expose you to an allegation that you failed to act with due skill, care and diligence. It may also potentially preclude you from establishing a 'reasonable steps' defence if you are alleged to have breached the duty of responsibility.

Scenario 5 (Executives only)

You have been made aware that one of your senior reports has repeatedly failed to undertake his mandatory computer-based training and to attend two professional development off-sites. He is also apparently 'relaxed' about the fact that a number of his direct reports have similarly failed to complete their mandatory training courses.

How do you respond?

Commentary

You must take reasonable steps to ensure that the business of the firm for which you are responsible is controlled effectively. In this scenario (and against that backdrop), you would be expected to have actively considered whether the relevant individual(s) are sufficiently competent and knowledgeable to continue to be able discharge their respective functions – in light of their failure to complete the mandatory training courses.

In any event, you should ensure that the individual(s) concerned complete all outstanding training at the earliest practicable opportunity. It should be made clear that failure to do so will likely result in disciplinary (and potentially financial) consequences. You should request an update from the relevant internal functions to track whether all training has indeed been satisfactorily completed by the specified deadline.

As a separate (albeit related) consideration, it should be noted that a firm's (and Senior Manager's) tolerance of a failure by certain individuals to complete mandatory training courses may well be perceived by the Regulator as indicative of cultural shortcomings. Clearly, this would not be a helpful impression for the Regulator to form, and could precipitate further and wider enquiries.

Scenario 6 (NEDs only)

You are attending a board meeting at which a significant prospective acquisition is being considered. After reading the board pack ahead of this meeting, you have some specific concerns regarding the timing and potential implications of the proposed transaction. You attempt to raise these concerns during the board meeting, but you feel that they are too readily discounted, without any substantive discussion.

Commentary

As a non-executive director, it is important that you are afforded a meaningful opportunity to raise any concerns and that these are properly discussed. In this scenario, you should request that the meeting minutes reflect your concerns and challenge.

Separately, you might express to the chairman your dissatisfaction with how this matter was handled at the board meeting, and reiterate that, in the future, you would expect your views and concerns to be given a proper airing.

Fundamentally, NEDs are expected to exercise demonstrable challenge and hold the Executive to account. Any perceived shortcomings in this regard could result in an allegation of failure to act with due skill, care and diligence.

Practical guidance

It is likely, if not inevitable, that the Regulator will wish to meet with certain Senior Managers during supervisory visits. While it is obviously impossible to predict the precise line of questioning or topics raised, Senior Managers might usefully consider how convincingly they could answer the following (non-exhaustive) set of questions:

- How many certified staff do you have within your area(s) of responsibility?
- Could you summarise the key conduct risks within your area(s) of responsibility?
- Could you summarise the 'fitness and propriety' assessment framework within your area(s) of responsibility?
- Could you summarise your key responsibilities (as per your Statement of Responsibilities)?
- Could you explain how your delegates are effectively overseen and monitored?
- Could you summarise the risk and control framework within your area(s) of responsibility?
- How do you ensure that/monitor whether employees within your area(s) of responsibility are acting in line with the firm's cultural and behavioural expectations?
- How do you continue to ensure that the systems and controls employed within your area(s) of responsibility remain fit for purpose?
- How do you ensure that the right 'tone from the middle' is set and maintained within your area(s) of responsibility?
- Can you summarise your regulatory obligations?
- Could you explain how the 3 Lines of Defence model operates and your role in that context?
- How do you promote good regulatory compliance within your area(s) of responsibility? Can you provide recent examples?
- Do you understand the interplay between your individual accountability and your responsibility for collective decisions?
- How do you ensure that you and your employees are (and remain) appropriately trained? What policies and procedures are in place for reviewing ongoing competence and performance?

10

CONCLUSION

This book has addressed the various avenues of potential regulatory exposure for Senior Managers – covering roles of both an executive and non-executive nature.

The continuing globlisation of financial regulation – largely a product of G20 commitments – has resulted in national regimes with common fundamental underpinnings and drivers. Accordingly, the essence of much of the practical guidance contained in this edition will be of utility to senior officers of financial institutions located or regulated in other prominent jurisdictions – including the United States.

With the advent of the SMR, increased use of attestations and the new-found threat of cultural attribution, the risk of personal regulatory liability has arguably never been greater for senior-level individuals within financial institutions.

Whichever enforcement route(s) the Regulator opts to pursue in any given case, the Senior Manager concerned will need to be well placed to counter any regulatory challenge. In practice, the Senior Manager will need to be able to demonstrate that he or she took reasonable steps in the particular circumstances. It is impossible (and, indeed, it would not be advisable) to be definitively prescriptive as to what would constitute such reasonable steps. However, it is hoped that this publication has provided an instructive indication of the types of measures that might most obviously serve to help with the establishment of reasonable steps. Indeed, if this guidance is heeded and the suggested mind-set adopted, Senior Managers should be well placed to respond to any adverse interest if they suddenly happen to find themselves under the regulatory spotlight.

In reality, the type of conduct that would have amounted to 'reasonable steps' pre-SMR is substantively similar to that required under the SMR. In other words, if a Senior Manager was acting responsibly and in line with prevailing regulatory expectations pre-SMR, then he or she should arguably not need to be materially adjusting his or her day-to-day conduct specifically for the purposes of the SMR (perhaps with the notable exception of the degree to which key decisions/discussions and delegate oversight are recorded).

Senior Managers may find it helpful to revisit periodically the tables in chapter 4 or 5 (as applicable) – to ensure that the key pointers remain at the forefront of their minds and are not forgotten.

It remains to be seen whether and how the Regulator will pursue more senior-level individuals. In light of the Regulator's very public commitment to bring more senior individuals to account, and its new weapon in the guise of the Duty of Responsibility (alongside Statements of Responsibilities and Responsibility Maps), increased personal enforcement activity might well be expected. However, as illustrated, Senior Managers can do much to help themselves and to mitigate this heightened perceived risk down to an acceptable level.